THE SOUL OF
SPIDER-MAN

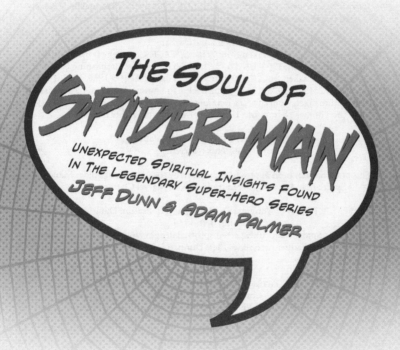

THE SOUL OF SPIDER-MAN

UNEXPECTED SPIRITUAL INSIGHTS FOUND
IN THE LEGENDARY SUPER-HERO SERIES

JEFF DUNN & ADAM PALMER

Regal

From Gospel Light
Ventura, California, U.S.A.

Published by Regal
From Gospel Light
Ventura, California, U.S.A.
www.regalbooks.com
Printed in the U.S.A.

All Scripture quotations, unless otherwise indicated, are taken from the *Holy Bible,*
New International Version®. Copyright © 1973, 1978, 1984 by International Bible Society.
Used by permission of Zondervan Publishing House. All rights reserved.

Other versions used are
THE MESSAGE—Scripture taken from *THE MESSAGE*. Copyright © by Eugene H.
Peterson, 1993, 1994, 1995. Used by permission of NavPress Publishing Group.
NASB—Scripture taken from the *New American Standard Bible,* © 1960, 1962, 1963,
1968, 1971, 1972, 1973, 1975, 1977 by The Lockman Foundation. Used by permission.
NKJV—Scripture taken from the *New King James Version*. Copyright © 1979, 1980, 1982
by Thomas Nelson, Inc. Used by permission. All rights reserved.

This book has not been approved or licensed by the creators of Spider-Man®.
Spider-Man® is a registered trademark of Marvel Characters, Inc.

Library of Congress Cataloging-in-Publication Data
Dunn, Jeff, 1959-
The soul of Spider-man : unexpected spiritual insights found in the legendary
super-hero series / Jeff Dunn, Adam Palmer.
p. cm.
ISBN 978-0-8307-4752-8 (trade paper)
1. Spider-Man (Fictitious character) 2. Comic books, strips, etc.—
Religious aspects—Christianity. I. Palmer, Adam, 1975- II. Title.
PN6728.S6D86 2010
741.5'973—dc22
2009049651

1 2 3 4 5 6 7 8 9 10 11 12 13 14 15 / 16 15 14 13 12 11 10

Rights for publishing this book outside the U.S.A. or in non-English languages
are administered by Gospel Light Worldwide, an international not-for-profit ministry.
For additional information, please visit www.glww.org, email info@glww.org, or write
to Gospel Light Worldwide, 1957 Eastman Avenue, Ventura, CA 93003, U.S.A.

To order copies of this book and other Regal products in bulk quantities,
please contact us at 1-800-446-7735.

DEDICATION

From Jeffrey Dunn:
To my son, Mark.

From Adam Palmer:
*For my children, who continually
hone my Spidey sense.*

CONTENTS

INTRODUCTION

For many of us, Spider-Man is the ultimate superhero. There have been times where one of the authors of this book (you'll have to guess which one) has extended a hand toward the remote control, lying on the table across the room, and, with an imaginary "thwip!" sent a make-believe bit of webbing from our wrist to retrieve it.

It didn't work, of course. But it's nice to pretend.

We love Spider-Man. We won't deny it.

We also love Jesus. We won't deny that, either. (In fact, we love Jesus more, but Spidey is the ultimate in superheroes.)

As authors, we've conditioned ourselves to look for the spiritual in everything. Especially modern stories. We love to try to figure out what the story is telling us about spirituality, eternity, good and evil. We even try to catch a glimpse of Jesus in the script and see if it says anything at all about the way He wants us to live our lives.

We do this because Jesus often used stories to illustrate His sermons. To make His points palatable. To demonstrate the way we should live. And if Jesus used stories, then we feel like we're on solid ground when we look into stories to find spiritual truths. We could even call them superhero parables! And believe us, we feel like there's a *lot* of spiritual truth in the Spider-Man mythology.

So here's the big question: What are we, as a culture, learning when we watch Peter Parker pull that mask over his head and go to work against the Green Goblin, Doctor Octopus, the Sandman, Venom and the parade of other small-time thieves and crooks he creams throughout the movie trilogy?* Are we just seeing entertainment, a bunch of flashing lights on a screen, or are we peering behind the curtain of society and seeing something else altogether?

Is it possible to find God in the lumbering belly of this two-and-a-half billion-dollar beast?

We think so. We see spiritual insights all through the *Spider-Man* trilogy. And that's why this book exists. To let you see what we see. To encourage you to look beyond the crazy-good special effects, the heart-stopping action, the sharp dialogue and Tobey Maguire's terrible crying, and touch the heart of God.

To find the hero within you.

Because it's in there. And it isn't waiting for any crazy, one-in-a-million shot in a science lab to unlock it, either. The hero within you is just waiting for you to learn the truth about yourself, about God and about the world around you.

Like Spider-Man, you'll find it amazing.

---

* In compiling this book, we made a deliberate decision very early on to stick to discussing only the *Spider-Man* films of 2002, 2004 and 2007. While the comics, the early campy movies with Nicolas Hammond as Peter and the various television incarnations of our favorite web-slinger are rich with spiritual material to mine, we didn't want to let our focus get too thin. So keep in mind, as we move ahead, that we're only talking about what we see in the first three films of the *Spider-Man* saga. Now get your DVDs ready, find a comfortable chair, pour yourself a soda and get ready to travel through the films with us to discover the soul of *Spider-Man*.

THE SOUL OF SPIDER-MAN

PART ONE

SPIDER-MAN (2002)

INT. COLUMBIA UNIVERSITY RESEARCH LAB - DAY*

PETER nervously approaches MARY JANE. She's finally
alone, admiring the fourteen genetically modified
spiders. He holds up his camera.

> **PETER**
> Can I take your picture?
> I need one with a student in it.

She's pleasantly surprised.

> **MARY JANE**
> Sure. Where do you want me?
> (indicates the spider enclosure)
> Over here?

> **PETER**
> (agreeing to anything)
> Yeah! Yeah, that's great.

Peter backs up a few steps and begins taking
pictures. He's standing in front of a TELEVISION
MONITOR that shows computer animation of the genetic
engineering process at the lab. Mary Jane awkwardly
gestures toward the spiders as she looks at the
camera. Snap. Snap.

Peter's enraptured at the idea of staring at the girl
of his dreams through the lens. At this moment, he

need not content himself with stolen glances. She is his. Snap. He keeps taking picture after picture, drawing the moment out.

                    PETER
               Perfect.

CU on: The fifteenth SPIDER, dizzyingly descending on a gossamer thread from a web built directly above Peter. It is red and blue and clearly intelligent.

Mary Jane improvises some stage business, living in the moment of semi-stardom. Peter keeps snapping. Snap. Snap.

The spider keeps coming. We see its POV as it gets closer and closer to the unaware Peter. It touches lightly on Peter's knuckle as his hand operates the camera, makes its way down his hand.

A female voice calls toward them. Another student.

                    VOICE (O.S.)
               MJ! Let's go!

Without a cursory glance at Peter, or a word of any kind, Mary Jane turns to leave, looking almost embarrassed at having been caught at the other end of the nerdy photographer's lens.

                    PETER
               (calling after her)
               Thanks.

ANGLE ON the spider, now near Peter's thumb.

ECU: the spider opens its maw wide and, with violence, plunges it deep into Peter's hand.

Shock! Peter is stunned and instinctively shakes his hand toward the floor. The spider falls off, and Peter watches it crawl away on the carpet. He examines the WOUND. It lies across a blood vessel and is already swelling, with two red dots indicating fang-marks. Peter looks simultaneously in pain and afraid.

TEACHER (O.S.)
Parker? Let's do it.

Peter looks up and walks out of frame. We stay on the television monitor just as it switches to animated DNA, showing parts of the double-helix ladder being replaced with different-colored parts, being made into a whole. The helix is wiped away by a picture of the genetically modified spider and these words: NEW SPECIES.

* This script was created as fiction by the authors and is not part of the actual *Spider-Man* movie or television script.

CHAPTER ONE

A NEW SPECIES

Let's be honest: Life gets old sometimes.

Even when something's new, it gets old. Ever gotten a present for Christmas or your birthday that you desperately wanted, only to grow tired of it in just a few hours, days or weeks? No matter how new that something is, the shininess always dulls, the newness wears off, and it just becomes another thing taking up space in your closet, destined to become a garage sale item someday.

We all encounter times in our lives when we feel like that used-up Christmas gift, when we feel like we're destined for the world's biggest garage sale. When we feel like we just don't belong or we're on the outside looking in.

Peter Parker is just such a kid.

But with a single spider bite, Peter Parker was no longer the nerd, the downtrodden, the beat-up. Ten minutes into the first *Spider-Man* movie, he becomes different; a change happens within him at a fundamental level.

Before this pivotal occurrence in his life, Peter Parker was fast on the road to geekdom. The glasses-wearing brainiac, the typical "science whiz," as Norman Osborn, his best friend's father, calls him, Peter was a regular ol' high school senior with a gigantic brain and dreams of becoming a professional photographer. What he was going to do with his smarts, we'll never know.

As the movie opens, we already know Peter's like us, on the outside looking in—a perspective demonstrated by Peter literally running alongside a school bus as everyone else laughs at him from inside.

Everyone but Mary Jane Watson, of course, who implores the driver to stop and pick him up. We can see at this point that Peter, if left on his own, would drown in the ocean of society. He is helpless *and* hopeless. He would still be able to carve out a life for himself, perhaps, but it would be a life lived under the thumb of bully Flash Thompson and other jerks like him, who rule the world with charisma, charm and muscles.

We all feel a little like Peter sometimes. This is why the Spider-Man story has caught on so well—we can all empathize with the guy. How he just wants to live his life and do his thing, but some outside influence (in Peter's case, torment from Flash & Co.) prevents us.

Sounds like David. Not King David, the powerful ruler, but the young shepherd boy David, whose story we start reading about in 1 Samuel 16. This is a guy God had big plans for, but that no one paid attention to.

Samuel, the big-time prophet of Israel, went to David's house on God's orders to anoint a king. Now, David had a ton of brothers, and they were all studlier than he was. He looked like a little kid, a nerdy little shepherd boy pounding on the side of his brothers' school bus, hoping they'd slow down to let him on. Samuel took one look at David's oldest brother Eliab and said to himself, "Here's the guy. Here's the king, the big superhero that's going to guard and protect and lead Israel."

"Nope," God said. "You're looking at the outside, but I'm looking at his heart. He's not our man."

Samuel moved on to the next brother, Abinadab. He was a stout fellow, we presume. Probably not as imposing as Eliab, but still a good candidate for king. "Ah," said Samuel to himself, "God's faking the people out by not taking that first one, but this is going to be the one."

"Nope," God said.

Next was David's brother Shammah.

"Nope."

"Come on, God," Samuel must've been thinking. "This is getting ridiculous."

In all, seven of David's brothers went before Samuel, and God rejected all of them. David's dad, Jesse, didn't even bring David up—took him out of the running before he was ever in it. Wrote him off.

God—and Samuel—wrote David back in. "Do you have any more sons?" Samuel asked Jesse. "God has rejected all these guys."

"Well," Jesse said, "there's the youngest, but, come on—he's tending the sheep."

Samuel sent for him, and the second David appeared, God said, "Yep. There's My guy."

So Samuel anointed him to be king over Israel, and that simple act, that anointing, changed David's life forever—and the change was put into action in the very next chapter in the Bible, when David went up against Israel's own supervillain, the Philistine Goliath.

But back to Peter Parker. When he's bitten by that genetically modified spider and that monitor flashes behind him, we're given an indication that Peter is changed into a new species. It isn't an outward change—he doesn't just put on muscles or get better vision without laser eye surgery—his DNA is changed. He is changed at the molecular level.

He becomes something completely new.

A new creation, if you will.

In 2 Corinthians 5:17, the Bible says, "Therefore, if anyone is in Christ, he is a new creation; the old has gone, the new has come!" Boy, that sounds really familiar.

No, Peter Parker doesn't become a Christian, but his transformation into Spider-Man is a wonderful parallel parable about the Christian life. When we accept Jesus' sacrifice, when we welcome Him into our hearts, He really does change us from the inside out.

We are no longer garage-sale material. We are no longer used-up versions of ourselves. We are changed from within to become something valuable, something new again—something that will *never* dull or lose value.

We all have that feeling at times in our lives: that innate sense that something in ourselves needs to change if we are going to move forward. We all feel like Peter, running alongside the bus of life, pounding on the side and hoping it'll stop long enough for us to jump on board.

Philosophers talk about the "God-shaped hole" that we each have inside of us. Remember that double helix in the television monitor, how it had gaps in it that were replaced to create a new species? It's like that. We have gaps within ourselves, holes in our souls that can only be filled by Jesus. By His love. By His sacrifice.

And when we accept that love, that sacrifice? We become a new creation. We kiss that old way of living goodbye. We stop running alongside the bus, pounding to get on, and we start swinging from skyscrapers, free to pursue life on God's terms, not man's.

We become super, because He has made us that way.

CHAPTER TWO

WITH GREAT POWER . . .

Powerlessness. It's one of the worst feelings in the world. And yet, it's something we all feel at one time or another. Something spins out of our control, or we wind up being subjected to authority we'd rather not subject ourselves to. Or we take a look at the ills of the world and feel like there's just *nothing* we can do— and in the meantime, the price of gasoline just keeps going up.

But is it true? Are we really powerless through and through?

Not according to Peter Parker. The grand refrain that echoes throughout the *Spider-Man* trilogy, and indeed throughout our hero's comic-book origins, are these words, spoken to Peter by his Uncle Ben: *With great power comes great responsibility.*

It's such a simple sentiment, but one that is packed with ramifications out the wazoo. It becomes Peter's touchstone, his anchor, the very reason he becomes Spider-Man in the first place. The words haunt him, and they're made all the more powerful by the death of the man who spoke them. They lead Peter to a jarring realization: He's been given a gift. A great gift. A gift of great power.

How is he going to use it?

He starts off using it for his own monetary gain, heading out to carve up wrestler Bone Saw McGraw in hopes of landing a cool three-Gs to buy a car and impress Mary Jane. In the ring, Peter runs circles around Bone Saw, dipping into his trademark sarcasm and generally getting full of himself. Yeah, he's feeling pretty good about this gift of great power. This is going to impress a lot of chicks.

Then the promoter gyps him and Peter decides to exact revenge by stepping aside, shirking the great responsibility that came with his great power. He allows a criminal to rob the promoter. Of course, Peter doesn't realize the pain his selfishness will cause.

That simple, selfish act leads to the death of his uncle. Peter wallows in his great power, skipping the "great responsibility" part, and doing so leads to unexpected heartache.

Believe it or not, though we often feel powerless, we do, in fact, have great power. The apostle Paul discussed the power available to Christians in Ephesians 1:18-21:

> I pray also that the eyes of your heart may be enlightened in order that you may know the hope to which he has called you, the riches of his glorious inheritance in the saints, and his incomparably great power for us who believe. That power is like the working of his mighty strength, which he exerted in Christ when he raised him from the dead and seated him at his right hand in the heavenly realms, far above all rule and authority, power and dominion, and every title that can be given, not only in the present age but also in the one to come.

We have great power, right there—the power that lies within a message of hope, a message of love and reconciliation. A message found throughout the Bible, in places like John 3:16 and Romans 3:23, where God specifically speaks to our hearts and tells us that He loves us and desires a relationship with us.

So the question is: What's *our* responsibility? What are *we* doing with the great power *we've* been given?

There have been a zillion books written about this power, and too often they point us in the direction of fulfilling our selfish desires. They go on and on about how we can live a great life full of prosperity and purpose and all-around awesomeness. These things aren't bad, of course, but when we hyper-focus on ourselves and the way Christianity benefits us and only us, we start to let our responsibility slip.

The fact remains that we have a responsibility that comes with our great power. We have a responsibility to care for those around us, as evidenced in James 1:27: "Religion God our Father accepts as pure and faultless is this: to look after orphans and widows in their distress and to keep oneself from being polluted by the world."

We have a responsibility to put our selfishness to the side and live humble lives, as we see in Philippians 2:3-4: "Do nothing out of selfish ambition or vain conceit, but in humility consider others better than yourselves. Each of you should look not only to your own interests, but also to the interests of others."

We have great power. What are we doing about the "responsibility" part? Are we shirking our responsibility and living a pre-dead-uncle life, living it up in a wrestling ring to score a few extra bucks and impress the girl of our dreams? Or are we taking the high road and looking to serve our fellow man?

Peter Parker eventually takes the high road, even when the going got tough. Newspaper chief J. Jonah Jameson and the *Daily Bugle* are squarely against him, calling Spider-Man a menace to the city and demanding his arrest, even when Spidey is doing good all over the place. Yet that doesn't deter Peter. He doesn't say, "Forget this mess, it isn't worth it." On the contrary, he just keeps doing what he knows he should do, regardless of what his detractors think. He takes his great responsibility seriously and gives to the city until it, quite literally, hurts.

The question remains: What will we do with our great power? Are we brave enough to follow in Spider-Man's footsteps?

With your great power comes a great responsibility. Are you up to the challenge?

BE CAREFUL WHO YOU CHANGE INTO

Have you ever changed your look, just for fun—say, cut your hair, switched to contact lenses or gotten your ears pierced? Maybe you didn't just change your look, but changed your lifestyle. Maybe you decided to eat healthier, or to start reading more nonfiction (good choice!) or to smile more.

Change can be a really good thing, especially if it's for the better. If you decide to change your driving habits to cut down on greenhouse gases, that's a good thing. If you decide to be kind to everyone you meet, that's a good change, too.

A lot of times, though, we change just because. Or we change without even realizing we are. We snap at our loved ones or step on the scale to find a disappointing number. We look at our lives and think, *How did I get here?*

Things are changing in Peter Parker's world. He *was* trying to figure out how to live a regular ol' life, and now he has to figure out something completely different: life with superpowers. And his shift in focus isn't always for the better. He's too busy exploring his new abilities to come home and paint the kitchen with Uncle Ben. He strings webbing through his room, starting with a Dr. Pepper can and ending with a smashed lamp. He finally fights back when Flash Thompson brings the pain—and makes quite a spectacle of it by punching Flash into next Thursday.

In short, Peter's dealing with far more than your standard adolescent angst. And he hasn't even started with all the Green-Goblin-fighting and Mary-Jane-rescuing stuff.

But Peter is sure of one thing: Even though his life is upside-down, topsy-turvy, he'll figure it out. He is certain that he doesn't need Uncle Ben's words of wisdom, especially a phrase he uncorks just seconds before the all-important "With great power comes great responsibility" mantra.

Uncle Ben looks at Peter and underscores the fact that teen-agerhood is a time of great change, even delivering a line that comes across as an in-joke to those of us watching the film ("I went through exactly the same thing at your age," to which Peter responds, "No, not exactly." Ha!). Uncle Ben acknowledges the changes Peter is undergoing (though he doesn't know the half of it) and reminds him: "Just be careful who you change into."

Why? Why would Uncle Ben caution such care in the change? Because he knows that Peter has a choice. It certainly looks like Peter is on a self-destructive path of violence, rebellion, apathy and self-centeredness—and in a way, he is. He's a little bit drunk on his own superpowers, and it's starting to show in his outward actions. He isn't antisocial, and he isn't turning into a supervillain, but he is preparing to use his superpowers in a way that benefits himself and only himself.

Uncle Ben sees it and gives Peter some invaluable wisdom . . . though we would argue that Uncle Ben doesn't take it far enough. In the film, Cliff Robertson delivers the dialogue superbly, and really makes us believe that Peter is at a time when he's "changing into the man he's going to become for the rest of his life." But in actuality, while adolescence does pave the way for adulthood, it is not irrevocable. If we make bad choices as teenagers, we aren't necessarily saddled with a crummy adult life; we are merely saddled with the consequences of bad choices, and the road to lasting happiness becomes more difficult.

Instead, every day is a decision. Every hour, every minute. We're constantly making decisions, either to do the right thing or the wrong thing or nothing. Our lives are in a constant state of change, whether it looks like it or not, and we are never guaranteed tomorrow.

So, the words ring true. "Be careful who you change into."

And they remind us of other words, spoken by God to the Israelites and recounted in Deuteronomy 30:19-20:

> This day I call heaven and earth as witnesses against you that I have set before you life and death, blessings and curses. Now choose life, so that you and your children may live and that you may love the LORD your God, listen to his voice, and hold fast to him. For the LORD is your life, and he will give you many years in the land he swore to give to your fathers, Abraham, Isaac and Jacob.

It's all about free will, when it comes to this life of ours. That's the way God set it up for us: He gave us the ability to choose. That's why the Tree of the Knowledge of Good and Evil was in the Garden of Eden in the first place: God wanted to make sure that obedience was a conscious decision Adam made, not a mandate handed down from on high. How could Adam choose to obey if he was surrounded by nothing but good? He had to have the ability to choose unwisely in order for his obedience to mean anything.

And in a way, we all have that same decision placed before us, at all times. We're all changing—but we have to be careful about who we're changing into. Are we, like scientist Norman Osborn, letting our fears and worries get the best of us and changing into horrible, selfish monsters hell-bent on seeing our own desires fulfilled, regardless of the price others have to pay?

Or are we, like Peter Parker, earnestly seeking to choose life—making choices that lead us to bettering ourselves and the world around us, acting selflessly in order to save others and make this world safer and more peaceful?

Who are we changing into? Regardless of the choices we've made in the past, we can start making the right choice. Today. Right now. We can decide *exactly* who we change into.

And we can make sure that person is worth the change.

BONE SAW

Doing something new can be rewarding. But at the same time, it can be downright scary. Especially if the new stuff we intend to do is difficult. How many times have you been about to undertake something difficult—maybe a new diet, or guitar lessons, or getting your driver's license—only to feel like the world is set against you?

Peter undertakes a new hobby, of sorts, when he gets his superpowers. But before he becomes our friendly neighborhood Spider-Man, he is The Human Spider, a kid in a homemade costume ready to do something new in a wrestling arena.

In the center of the massive space is a ring, and in that, stalking the boards, is Bone Saw, his formidable opponent. Bone Saw is adored by the massive throng of cheering fans, many of whom are carrying handmade signs singing his praises with phrases like "Bone Saw: Master of Disaster" and "File Under *D* for *Dead*." The emcee also sings the praises of Bone Saw, the "Titan of Testosterone."

Peter heads down to register and is greeted with more confidence . . . in Bone Saw. The registrar even tries to convince Peter that he shouldn't wrestle, but Peter won't have it. He is committed to seeing this thing through, because he has his eyes on that $3,000 prize. He has to get that car so he can impress Mary Jane!

The announcer, marvelously portrayed by the great Bruce Campbell (trivia: Campbell is also the sneering usher who won't let Peter see MJ in *The Importance of Being Earnest* in *Spider-Man 2* and the maitre-d' who helps Peter propose in *Spider-Man 3*), rubs salt in the wound when he tells Peter that his wrestling moniker, "The Human Spider," sucks. The announcer does him a favor and dubs him "Spider-Man" when he introduces Peter to the bloodthirsty fans.

Peter begins to walk down the ramp and is greeted by Bone Saw's entourage of female friends, all of whom share his proclivity for witty repartee, throwing derogatory remarks at Peter like Peyton Manning throws deep passes. To wit:

"Bone Saw's going to eat you up and spit you out, little man."

"I hope you brought your mommy with you, 'cause you're going to need someone to go crying to."

"We're gonna break you."

"I'm gonna rip all eight of your feeble legs off one by one."

And so on.

Then, adding further to the trepidation, just as Peter approaches the ring, a previous challenger is wheeled by on a gurney, groaning about how he can't feel his leg.

Oh, yeah . . . *then* Peter sees a giant sign being held up in the crowd: "KILL HIM!"

Our hero must be simply *brimming* with confidence. Especially when iron bars swing down from the ceiling and Peter is locked into a cage with Bone Saw, who informs him: "You're going nowhere. I got you for three minutes of playtime." Peter's fear is palpable as he pleads with the officials to open up the cage—this is *not* what he signed up for.

All signs point to disaster.

The devil does this sort of thing all the time. He is hard at work to convince us that his power is greater than God's . . . that, when it comes right down to it, we just better give up and give in, because there's no way we'll ever succeed at anything worthwhile. This is why the apostle Paul cautioned us not to become weary as we do good (see Galatians 6:9). He wouldn't have said anything about it if he didn't know that we'd feel that way sometimes.

Paul also used a lot of imagery in his epistles about life being like a race (see 1 Corinthians 9:24; Galatians 5:7; 2 Timothy 4:7). He understood that this is a life that is meant to be lived out, one foot in front of the other, despite the obstacles. Running a race doesn't come easily—you have to fight through pain, fatigue, sweat, the weather and other competitors who may seek to do you active harm. And yet, we're all supposed to run.

A biblical comparison to the story of Peter Parker and Bone Saw can be found in Matthew 14, when Jesus walked on the actual waters of a lake to reach His disciples, who were already in a boat and headed across. The disciples freaked out, thinking it must be a ghost walking toward them, so Jesus tried to calm them down by hollering out who He was.

Peter, one of His disciples, decided to test the waters, if you will, and said, "If it's really You, then tell me to come walk on the water toward You."

Jesus did. And Peter hopped out of the boat and started strutting his stuff on top of the water. Pretty cool, eh?

But then Peter noticed that it was kind of windy outside, and there were a lot of waves around, and *Gee, it sure is tough going, and uh oh, I'm starting to sink!* (See v. 30.)

Something to think about: Why would Peter stress about the wind? Why is *that* the thing that caused him to sink?

Let's turn this around. If the water was as still as glass, would he have *then* been able to walk on it? Was it the wind that prevented Peter from using his gift from God, or was it his own self-doubt?

Peter fell into a trap many of us do: He took his eyes off the gift he'd been given, the task he'd been told to do—by Jesus Himself, mind you—and focused them on something that had absolutely nothing to do with what was within him. And in so doing, he lost his faith.

The other Peter, Peter Parker, experiences a similar thing. He focuses his eyes on his outside circumstances—the crowd, the taunts of Bone Saw's minions, the cage and the trash-talk of Bone Saw himself—and begins to doubt his own abilities. As viewers, we know that Peter is going to handle himself in that ring, but in the midst of the situation, Peter forgets what he can do . . . and it freaks him out.

He begins to sink, just a little.

But he remembers himself in the nick of time, and emerges triumphant over what appeared to be a very unbeatable foe. He stops listening to the negative messages that surround him and starts listening to his own heart, remembering who he is and what a tremendous gift he's been given.

And that's all it takes. He finishes that particular race. He goes into that ring as Peter Parker, but he perseveres and comes out The Amazing Spider-Man.

So before you change your eating habits or start training for that marathon or buckle in for your driver's test, prepare yourself for the inevitable onslaught of negative voices, telling you that you can't do it. And then further prepare yourself to ignore those voices and listen instead to what Jesus is telling you: "Don't be afraid. It's Me. Come walk on the water."

CHAPTER FIVE

THE GREENNESS OF GREED

What does it mean to be greedy? Does it mean you're a person who thirsts for money like an extreme surfer thirsts after Mountain Dew? Or does greed go deeper than that?

We get an example of greed in Norman Osborn, as he undergoes his sad, sad transformation into the Green Goblin. Here we have a man who clearly loves his son, though he has difficulty showing it. He also clearly loves the company he built, partly because it represents his life's work, and partly because it allows him to live in the opulence and luxury that come with being quite possibly the richest man in the world (gigantic mansions in the middle of New York City don't come cheap).

At the beginning of the film, Norman is a wealthy businessman who has accumulated considerable wealth through highly lucrative government weapons contracts. His company, Oscorp, has been working on a prototype for the military: a super-suit of body armor, that super-cool flying glider and the super-green strength-enhancing serum (or whatever scientific mumbo-jumbo they concocted to explain the green smoke).

Ah, but there is a snag, if you recall. The strength enhancers aren't working properly, and the researchers are going to have to "take it back to formula," in which case they will lose the contract.

What's a multi-billionaire research scientist to do?

Test it on himself . . . duh.

Norman is pushed forward by greed. He wants more and more and more. This greed is motivated by fear—a fear that somehow he won't have enough. He doesn't want to lose the contract to Quest Aerospace, because he fears that his business won't recover. And he can't stand to have his business falter. So rather than reevaluate his business model or refocus his corporation on other contracts or at least work on selling the glider and armor to the government and calling the serum a wash, he gets greedy.

Norman wants the whole kit and kaboodle, so he locks himself in that plexiglass room, breathes in the wicked green smoke and, after smashing up the place and killing his assistant, starts down the road to Green Goblinhood.

All because of greed.

He could have avoided it. And once he becomes the Goblin, he doesn't have to keep it up. He could come to his senses, could start doing the right thing, could turn himself in to the authorities for the murder of his assistant. But instead, he takes out the key players at Quest Aerospace, creating havoc in their company and with their program, removing their capability to receive the contract from the government and sending it Oscorp's way.

Even after that, he could still salvage himself and save a lot of bloodshed by coming clean when he has his next board meeting. But no. The board votes to sell the company . . . to Quest. Oh, and they make Norman resign, too. (He's not a real fan of life by this point.)

But he finds a way to get back at the board members, oh yes. He dresses up as the Goblin and bombs 'em at that big festival with all the balloons and Macy Gray. And that's where he is introduced to the man who will become his nemesis: Spider-Man.

From one thing to the next, Norman lets his greed make his decisions for him, and it ultimately leads to his downfall. Little by little, he lives out what we see in James 1:13-15:

When tempted, no one should say, "God is tempting me." For God cannot be tempted by evil, nor does he tempt anyone; but each one is tempted when, by his own evil desire, he is dragged away and enticed. Then, after desire has conceived, it gives birth to sin; and sin, when it is full-grown, gives birth to death.

Norman is tempted to give in to his basest desire: in his case, greed. And once he gives in to that temptation, that desire to succeed by cutting corners and taking risks, it gives birth to sin. Norman then nurses his sin, personified in the Green Goblin, and that persona leads him to his eventual death.

It isn't one wrong turn that leads Norman down the wrong path—it is the continual pursuit of greed, the non-stop focus on making wrong turn after wrong turn.

One can't help but think of the story of David and Bathsheba, when King David made one bad choice after another until he was confronted with his sin. We find this story in 2 Samuel 11, where it all begins with David doing a little slacking off from the job of being king. Instead of being out at the wars with all his loyal soldiers, he was hanging out at the palace, presumably sipping blueberry-almond smoothies and taking late-night strolls on the palace rooftop . . . where he spied the beautiful Bathsheba in a moment of repose (see v. 2).

Now, David had plenty of wives and other women at his disposal. But greed—the fear he might miss out on something—took hold. His sinful nature got the better of him, and he used his kingly authority to invite Bathsheba for a sleepover. She got pregnant, which was bad for David because . . . she was married. And her husband was off at the wars. Where David was supposed to be.

So what did David do? Come clean, beg for God's mercy? Nope. He told the captain of his army to send Bathsheba's husband, Uriah, home to his wife, pronto, so that he could spend some quality time with her and let nature take its course. And then they would all pretend the baby was Uriah's.

Except Uriah was too darn noble. He came back to Jerusalem, but refused even to go into his house, instead sleeping at the entrance with all his servants. David asked him what the deal was, and Uriah twisted the knife: "The ark and Israel and Judah are staying in tents, and [the commander of the army] and my lord's men are camped in the open fields. How could I go to my house to eat and drink and lie with my wife?" (v. 11).

Ouch.

His little ploy didn't work, so David got desperate—and that's when things got tragic. He told his army commander to send Uriah to the bloodiest part of the battle, then leave him high and dry so that he would be killed in the fighting.

After Uriah's death, David claimed Bathsheba as his own wife. She had the kid, a boy, and everything looked like it was going to turn out all right. Sure, Uriah died needlessly, but David's sin was covered up, right?

Not so fast. God saw the whole thing, and He was very, very displeased. God sent Nathan the prophet to David with a message, and his words (recorded in 2 Samuel 7–10) were harsh indeed:

> I anointed you king over Israel, and I delivered you from the hand of Saul. I gave your master's house to you, and your master's wives into your arms. I gave the house of Israel and Judah. And if all this had been too little, I would have given you even more. Why did you despise the word of the LORD by doing what is evil in his eyes? You struck down Uriah the Hittite with the sword and took his wife to be your own. You killed him with the sword of the Ammonites. Now, therefore, the sword will never depart from your house, because you despised me and took the wife of Uriah the Hittite to be your own.

And then David's son, the illegitimate one conceived in sin with Bathsheba, died.

This is serious stuff, sin. For Norman Osborn, it was greed. For King David, it was lust. What is it for you? Is there anything you need to take a cold, hard look at? Something you need to stop now, before it gets tragic?

Greed isn't just about money. We can be greedy in other areas of our lives—in relationships, in the ways we look at others, in our bad habits . . . the list goes on. It takes in anything that we are afraid to be without. But if we feed our greediness, we put ourselves on a dangerous road and often wind up like poor Norman Osborn.

The question remains: What are you going to do with your own greed, your own sin? The answer is completely up to you. Here's hoping you choose wisely.

OUR GOBLIN NATURE

So there you are, in your favorite store: just browsing, killing time . . . when you see your most favorite thing in the world *on sale!* You hadn't planned on buying anything, and you don't really have the extra cash to spend, but you really want it and so, ignoring your better nature, you buy it.

Impulse shopping is just one real-world example of something we all struggle with: the internal conflict between right and wrong. The ever-present angel and devil on our shoulders, each trying to convince us that *their* logic is the best logic.

Norman Osborn experiences this internal conflict—literally. He starts off normal. Well, as normal as greedy bazillionaires get. He has loads of money, and the house and car and servants and driver to show for it. Sure, he has his runaway ambition, left unchecked by morality . . . but at least he has a Rolls Royce to go with it. His ambition can run away in *style*.

Enter the super-soldier green gas ("performance enhancers" in the movie), and suddenly formerly normal Norman is hearing voices. Well, *a* voice. His own. Saying crazy things. Thanks to better-than-necessary acting by Willem Dafoe, we get to see Norman undergo this transformation, made all the creepier when he talks to himself in the mirror, switching back and forth from helpless Norman Osborn to the snarling, malignant, downright evil incarnation of the Green Goblin.

In this poignant scene, we finally get the gist of what's really going on with Norman. Like Smeagol/Gollum in the film version of *Lord of the Rings: The Two Towers*, Mr. Osborn is a creature at war with himself, a being who is letting his sinful, base nature take charge over a weaker opponent: his will to do good.

Norman is shocked to hear the voice of the Goblin cackling in his ear, and even tries to fool himself into thinking that it isn't him, a charge the Goblin tosses aside with a simple "Don't play the innocent with me." Even though the good part of him is appalled at the Goblin's actions, Norman is still culpable for them.

Still, the man is so addled at what's going on that he tells his Goblin self that he doesn't understand what's going on. In fact, he has to turn to the morning newspaper to discover the fact that, yes, he did indeed kill the Oscorp board members at the World Unity Festival.

Cowering at the full weight of his Goblin-ness, Norman first expresses horror at their deaths, and then resignedly allows the Goblin to take over more and more emotional real estate until he becomes mortal enemies with Spider-Man.

But look at Norman's face: bewildered, shaking his head as if he doesn't want to contemplate it, while the Goblin dementedly tells him in the mirror that the only solution is to deal with Spider-Man. It is plain that he doesn't want to do it, that he's appalled at what he's done thus far . . . and yet he is powerless to stop the Goblin.

(Just to make sure we're all on the same page here: Norman Osborn and the Goblin are not two different people. They are the same person, just different extensions of his personality. So when we say "Norman" or "the Goblin," we're talking about the same guy, but using those as reference points so you know which *aspect* of that guy we mean.)

You can see in his face that Norman is not looking forward to dealing with Spider-Man. And it reminds us, oddly enough, of Judas Iscariot, the man who betrayed Jesus for 30 pieces of silver.

Here is a man who sold his soul for a little money, who sold out all he believed in to gain some material wealth. A man who walked with Jesus Himself, in the flesh, yet allowed himself to be used by the devil to orchestrate Jesus' demise.

We see in Luke 22 that Judas, one of the 12 disciples closest to Jesus, had a dark side. Check out verses 3-6:

> Then Satan entered Judas, called Iscariot, one of the Twelve. And Judas went to the chief priests and the officers of the temple guard and discussed with them how he might betray Jesus. They were delighted and agreed to give him money. He consented, and watched for an opportunity to hand Jesus over to them when no crowd was present.

Judas struck a deal. His desire for money got in the way of his desire to do good. He let the devil have his way in him, following through with the plan: identifying Jesus in the Garden of Gethsemane with a kiss, betraying Him and sending Him to the cross.

But the guilt that came with acting on his greed was too much for Judas, something we read about in another of the Gospels:

> When Judas, who had betrayed [Jesus], saw that Jesus was condemned, he was seized with remorse and returned the thirty silver coins to the chief priests and the elders. "I have sinned," he said, "for I have betrayed innocent blood."
>
> "What is that to us?" they replied. "That's your responsibility."
>
> So Judas threw the money into the temple and left. Then he went away and hanged himself (Matthew 27:3-5).

Brutal consequences for giving in to sin.

And something to notice, both in the tale of Judas's betrayal of Jesus and in Norman Osborn's conversation with his Goblin self: In both cases, the more innocent side—the side that wants to do good—is goaded into doing something evil. That's the economy of the evil side: Doing evil deeds is fun, but corrupting the innocent is really, *really* fun. Double whammy.

This is the way sin works. The devil will convince you that the sinful way is the right way to go, and then, once you go down it and experience the inevitable remorse, he will say, "What is that to me? That's your responsibility."

Or, to put it another way: "Don't play the innocent with me."

Evil things almost always look better on *this* side of engaging in them. Sin is always fun for a short time—we're not going to deny that. Sin is often *fun*.

At first.

But the more you engage, the less fun it becomes. And the more enslaved to it you become.

Instead of indulging your goblin nature to the point of becoming a slave to it, look instead to God's nature. Instead of letting the devil have his way with you like he did with Judas, take a stand against the temptations of sin, knowing that, according to 1 Corinthians 10:13, "no temptation has seized you except what is common to man. And God is faithful; he will not let you be tempted beyond what you can bear. But when you are tempted, he will also provide a way out so that you can stand up under it."

You don't have to be ruled by the goblin within. There's always a way out.

Seek that way out, and you'll do something that Spider-Man did, too: defeat the Goblin.

THE SITUATION

That Mary Jane Watson sure knows how to holler at the absolute worst times. There she is, hanging on to Spider-Man for dear life as he is being pulled in two directions—one hand clutching his super-strong webbing strand, the other holding a cable car full of kids who were, apparently, sightseeing. In the dead of night. Okay.

And all Mary Jane can do is scream her head off. Not really helping much there, MJ.

Perhaps we should back up a bit. We are, of course, in the midst of the climactic rescue sequence toward the end of the first *Spider-Man* movie, just before Spidey and Gobby have their Battle Royale in that abandoned whatever-it-is, the place with all the dirt and decrepit brick walls that fall down easily.

You'll recall the way Spidey got into this rock-and-hard-place mess: through the Green Goblin's nefarious machinations (yes, you're welcome to use Nefarious Machinations as the name of your band, provided you pay us a quarter every time someone says it). The Goblin kidnaps Mary Jane, takes her to the top of the bridge and, just as she's waking up, blows up that station thing that holds the cable to the car full of late-night kid tourists.

The Goblin grabs the cable in one of his super-strong hands and holds Mary Jane in the other one. Lo and behold, here comes our hero, The Amazing Spider-Man! (One assumes the Green Goblin sent him an invitation in the mail: "Dear Spidey: Meet me at midnight, on top of that one bridge. I'll bring the snacks. *Don't be late!* Love, G.G.")

Using his very cool elastic-like webbing to vault himself to the bridge, Spider-Man shows up and faces down his nemesis . . . only to get treated to a little speechifying by the guy in green armor. To wit: "This is why only fools are heroes. Because you never know when some lunatic will come along with a sadistic choice: Let die the woman you love . . . or suffer the little children. Make your choice, Spider-Man, and see how a hero is rewarded."

Quite the little setup, no?

Mary Jane loses her slippers, and as we watch them tumble, we get the idea: *This is a long way down.* And also, *she's never going to get those slippers back.*

"We are who we choose to be," the Goblin intones. "Now *choose!*"

And with that, he lets go of both the cable car and Mary Jane, and we're treated to the iconic shot of each reflected in the eyepieces of Spider-Man's mask: Mary Jane on the left, the cable car on the right.

There is some truth to the Goblin's words: We really are who we choose to be. Our lives are the sum of our choices. And, just like the Green Goblin, there's something the devil loves to do: take a lie and put a sheen of truth on it.

We can see this in the life of Jesus, in Matthew 4, when the devil tempted Jesus to sin. Jesus had just undergone a 40-day fast when the devil approached and suggested, "Hey, You're hungry and You're the Son of God, right? Turn these stones into bread and get Your grub on" (see v. 3).

Hunger. That's a real thing. We do need food. And it's not fun to be hungry—why wouldn't it be okay to do that? Go ahead and make some bread?

But Jesus countered with actual truth: "It is written: 'Man does not live on bread alone, but on every word that comes from the mouth of God.'" For the record, He was quoting Deuteronomy 8:3.

Then the devil tried again, after taking Jesus to the highest point of the Temple (sort of like standing on the top of a bridge, isn't it?) and telling Him to toss Himself off the top, trusting that God would "command his angels concerning you, and they will lift you up in their hands, so that you will not strike your foot against a stone." The devil had the audacity to try out Jesus' own tactic on Him, quoting Psalm 91:11-12 as a means to get Jesus to go through with it.

See? It's a lie, spiffed up with truth. Words from Scripture are presented out of context, dressed up to look like perfect spiritual logic. But look at the way Jesus sidestepped the contest with some deeper truth from Deuteronomy 6:16, presented in its proper context: "It is also written: 'Do not put the Lord your God to the test.'"

One more. The devil then took Jesus to a high mountain and showed off the splendor of the kingdoms of the world, promising to give them all to Jesus in exchange for one simple thing: bowing down and worshiping him. Easy enough, huh?

Of course here, the devil has tipped his hand; it isn't even a temptation anymore. Jesus whipped out this verse from Deuteronomy 6:13: "Away from me, Satan! For it is written: 'Worship the Lord your God, and serve him only.'" The devil got too greedy and got his tail handed to him.

The same thing happens to the Green Goblin, eventually. He tries to present an ultimatum to Spider-Man—either Mary Jane or the cable car of kids will kiss the ground—but Spidey doesn't even acknowledge the Goblin's presentation of the situation. Instead, Spider-Man goes back to what he knows—his skill as a superhero—and finds himself stretched between the bridge and the cable car, with Mary Jane hollering in his ear (until, of course, he convinces her to climb down to the car, probably just so she can scream at the air instead of in his ear).

Spider-Man doesn't accept the world as the Goblin tries to present it, and as a result, he saves the day for Mary Jane and the cable car full of kids (it took a little help from some bystanders, who pelt the Goblin with tire irons and such when things are at their worst. Where, by the way, are those bystanders in *Spider-Man 3*, when our hero is getting the stuffing beaten out of him by Sandman and Venom?).

The devil will try to convince you that things are worse than they are. He will try to get in your head. He will try to get you to see the world *his* way, insinuating that all hope is lost. Don't buy it. Not for a second. Instead, do what Jesus did: Head back to the Word of God and read up on the *real* truth.

Part Two

Spider-Man 2 (2004)

INT. PETER'S APARTMENT - NIGHT*
A pajama-clad PETER sits in bed, eyes unfocused. We
slowly zoom in on his eyes as LIGHTNING flashes outside.
We can hear Peter's thoughts, and they include the
voice of UNCLE BEN, who is speaking as we...

DISSOLVE TO:
INT. UNCLE BEN'S CAR - DAY
It is a reprise of the scene in the first film, with
Peter and Uncle Ben sitting in the car, having a
chat. Outside the windows, the world is WHITE.

                    UNCLE BEN
          All the things you've been thinking about,
                    Peter, make me sad.

                      PETER
      Can't you understand? I'm in love with Mary Jane.

                    UNCLE BEN
      Peter, all the times we've talked of honesty,
      fairness, justice—all of those times I counted
          on you to have the courage to take those
                  dreams out into the world.

                      PETER
          I can't live your dreams anymore.
              I want a life of my own.

UNCLE BEN
You've been given a gift, Peter.
With great power comes great responsibility.
(reaches for Peter's hand)
Take my hand, son.

Peter regards the extended hand, conflicted. Should
he take it or shouldn't he? Uncle Ben looks into
Peter's eyes, offering the road of responsibility.

Peter decides with a broken heart and eyes full of tears.

PETER
No, Uncle Ben. I'm just Peter Parker.
I'm Spider-Man no more. No more.

DISSOLVE TO:
INT. PETER'S APARTMENT - CONTINUOUS
Peter is still prone in bed. We zoom in on his eyes
again as he says with resolution...

PETER
No more.

CUT TO:
EXT. BACK ALLEY - LATER

Peter, now dressed in his regular clothes, approaches
a TRASH CAN while holding his SPIDER-MAN SUIT. With
great determination, he drops it in, considers a moment, then walks away.

We pan down to the trash can to see the famous suit,
empty of its usual occupant, looking small and weak as
Peter recedes into the distance. He has made his choice.

CONTROL PROBLEMS

It's easy to feel like life is getting out of control. Deadlines come and go. You get let go from your job. Bills pile up. And then there's tomorrow, when it starts all over again.

Peter Parker, college student, knows how you feel. You ever wonder what his major is? Physics? Chemistry? Computer engineering?

We know what his major *isn't*: planning.

"Planning," says Dr. Connors, "is not a major at this university."

Peter has problems. He isn't getting to his classes, and when he does show up, he shows up late. He has good intentions about completing his schoolwork, but he can't seem to get his assignments done. And if he doesn't do a great job on his next paper—an interview with Doctor Otto Octavius—he will fail Dr. Connors's class.

Peter's tardiness is not just evident at school. As a deliveryman for Joe's Pizza, he has to uphold Joe's "29 Minutes Or It's Free" guarantee. He arrives late to work—again—and has only 8 minutes to go 42 blocks to deliver 8 large deep-dish pizzas. Even though he dons his Spidey costume and swings through Manhattan, he still gets to the customer 1 minute late. That's the last straw for Mr. Aziz, who fires Peter from his much-needed delivery job.

Then J. Jonah Jameson fires Peter from the *Bugle*. Well, okay, Jameson does that all the time. Still, Peter has to resort to presenting a photograph of Spider-Man—which he knows Jameson will misuse—in order to get paid. And the pay doesn't cover the advance he has already received. And with no money, Peter can't pay his rent—which makes Mr. Ditkovich, his landlord, very unhappy.

In short, Peter's life is not going so hot right now.

Spider-Man can do many things. He can grab a flying police car with his web, keeping it from flattening a crowd of people on the sidewalk. He can catch bad guys and stick them in a web to await the cops. He even has time to swing two children out of the path of an oncoming truck. Spidey has superhero powers that enable him to do many supernatural things. But there are some things he cannot do.

Such as get Peter to show up on time to class and to work. Or help Peter be responsible in his schoolwork. There are some occasions when superheroes are just powerless.

Maybe you feel like this sometimes. And maybe, in the midst of your life's craziness, you have been looking for Spider-Man to show up to save the day for you. If so, you are looking in the wrong place.

Just where should you look?

Try the floor. Go on—get a good, close look at it . . . say, by kneeling down. And while you're on your knees, pour out your complaints to God. Let Him know the troubles you are carrying. Don't try to sound religious, or act as if you are intruding on something more important God was doing. He cares for you. Really.

David was king over the kingdom of Israel, and he encountered many problems. Some just came with the territory: political challenges, wars to fight, economic balance to maintain. Other problems were brought on by his disobedience to God. But one thing remained constant in David's life: When he was in trouble, he turned to God.

Listen to these snippets of prayers from David as he was going through hard times:

> When I call, give me answers. God, take my side! Once, in a tight place, you gave me room; now I'm in trouble again: grace me! hear me! (Psalm 4:1, *THE MESSAGE*).

Listen, God! Please, pay attention! Can you make sense of these ramblings, my groans and cries? King-God, I need your help (Psalm 5:1, *THE MESSAGE*).

Keep me safe, O God, I've run for dear life to you. I say to God, "Be my Lord!" Without you, nothing makes sense (Psalm 16:1, *THE MESSAGE*).

Can you see David, the mighty warrior king of Israel, on his knees pleading for God's help? He had nowhere else to turn but to God. The same goes for us. When all looks lost, when it seems like life is piling up on us, when we just cannot go one more day, God is still God. By calling on Him for help, we acknowledge a simple truth:

He is God and we are not.

Consider the difference between daytime and nighttime. During the day, you are awake, in charge of your actions, your thoughts, all that you do. You are in control. But then at night, there is a shift. You lie down for sleep, and slowly you give up control. You don't control your tossing and turning, you don't decide what form your dreams will take. You have moved from control to faith—faith that you will be kept safe through the night and wake up once again in the morning.

The trick lies in learning to let go of control during the daylight hours as well. We are called to live by faith at all hours, not just while we are sleeping.

Peter Parker seeks to live in faith—faith in Spider-Man. But his Spidey powers often let him down just when he needs them. Here is good news: God will never let us down. He always comes through for us.

Start on your knees. Tell Him how out-of-control your life is just now. Don't look for help from a superhero. Trust in the One who is greater than all.

SPIDEY IN LOVE

Love does not make sense. It doesn't today, and it didn't 3,000 years ago when the wise Agur wrote these words:

> There are three things which are too wonderful for me, four which I do not understand: The way of an eagle in the sky, the way of a serpent on a rock, the way of a ship in the middle of the sea, and the way of a man with a maid (Proverbs 30:18-19, *NASB*).

Love between a man and a woman is not easy to understand; sometimes it is not even easy to detect. Is Peter Parker in love with Mary Jane Watson? Who knows? He sure doesn't.

"Tell us about yourself, Peter," asks Rosie Octavius. "Do you have a girlfriend?"

"Uh, well . . . I really don't know," says Peter.

Even Spider-Man has trouble with love.

Dr. Octavius knows a thing or two about love: "Love should never be a secret. If you keep something as complicated as love stored up inside, it can make you sick." Wow. For a scientist, he sure does know something about the human heart.

We humans were made in the image of God. We read in the Bible that God is love (see 1 John 4:16) and that out of this love He gave His only Son (see John 3:16). Since we are made to resemble God, it is in our nature to love and to give as well. If we don't, if we keep love bottled up on the inside, it can make us sick. Remember, God said at the very beginning that it is not good for man to be by himself. God created man and woman to be a couple, a team, to be more than two individuals. God created them to become one.

Love is a very strong emotion. Love for others motivated Mother Teresa to care for others for most of her life. Love for children keeps parents seeking the best for a rebellious child. And love can keep a man and woman together through desperately hard times.

But love is not an easy emotion to control.

"I finally got lucky in love," says Otto.

"We both did," his wife gently corrects. "But it's hardly perfect. You have to work at it."

We are all selfish by nature, some more than others, but all of us have the selfishness gene in our makeup. So while it may seem easy to give of ourselves during courtship, after we say "I do," it becomes harder. Rosie Octavius is right: Even the greatest of relationships is not perfect, and it takes constant work to keep it going.

C. S. Lewis wrote a whole book on love, which he called *The Four Loves*. In it, he has this to say about how long the feelings of love can last:

> Can we be in this selfless liberation for a lifetime? Hardly for a week. Between the best possible lovers this high condition is intermittent. The old self soon turns out to be not so dead as he pretended—as after a religious conversion. In either he may be momentarily knocked flat; he will soon be up again; if not on his feet, at least on his elbow, if not roaring, at least back to his surly grumbling or his mendicant whine.[1]

But back to Peter. He listens to the stories Otto and Rosie share about how they met, how they fell in love. It involved some reading of T. S. Eliot, a poet from the first half of the twentieth century. Otto says Eliot is hard to understand (a position shared by your humble authors), but recommends that Peter find some poetry to read with the one he loves.

Knowing that you, just like Peter, will eventually meet that one true love, we want you to be prepared. Thus, we offer the following love poems for your use. You can thank us later.

Sonnet XLIII
Elizabeth Barrett Browning

> How do I love thee? Let me count the ways.
> I love thee to the depth and breadth and height
> My soul can reach, when feeling out of sight
> For the ends of Being and ideal Grace.
> I love thee to the level of every day's
> Most quiet need, by sun and candlelight.
> I love thee freely, as men strive for Right;
> I love thee purely, as they turn from Praise.
> I love thee with the passion put to use
> In my old griefs, and with my childhood's faith.
> I love thee with a love I seemed to lose
> With my lost saints—I love thee with the breath,
> Smiles, tears, of all my life!—and, if God choose,
> I shall but love thee better after death.

A Red, Red Rose
Robert Burns

> O my Love's like a red, red rose,
>   That's newly sprung in June;
> O my Love's like the melody
>   That's sweetly played in tune.

As fair art thou, my bonnie lass,
        So deep in love am I;
And I will love thee still, my Dear,
        Till a' the seas gone dry.

Till all the seas gone dry, my Dear,
        And the rocks melt wi' the sun:
I will love thee still, my Dear,
        While the sands o' life shall run.

And fare thee well, my only Love!
        And fare thee well, a while!
And I will come again, my Love,
        Tho' it were ten thousand mile!

The heart has its reasons that reason knows nothing of.
—Blaise Pascal, *Pensées*

Without love, what are we worth?
Eighty-nine cents! Eighty-nine cents worth
of chemicals walking around lonely.
—Hawkeye, *M*A*S*H*

At the touch of love, everyone becomes a poet.
—Plato

Those who try to explain love between a guy and a girl are
fighting a losing battle. And if romantic love is hard to explain,
how could we ever hope to make sense of the greatest act of love
ever shown?

What is the greatest act of love ever shown, you ask? There
has never been a greater show of love than when God sent His
only Son, Jesus, to suffer and die in our place. Truly, there can be

no greater act of love than this. And at least to us, two guys who aren't all that good at higher math, it makes about as much sense as nuclear fusion.

If someone were to roll a hand grenade into a room where you and we, Adam and Jeff, were sitting, either of us would gladly jump on the bomb to save your life. (Every reader is precious to us!) But we're sorry—if that same hand grenade were rolled into that same room, neither of us could take his son (for Adam, it's Noah; for Jeff, it's Mark) and throw him on the grenade to save your life. We just could not do that.

And yet that is what God did for us. He took His only Son and cast Him on the cross to save our lives. It's awesome, it's unbelievably incredible . . . and it makes no logical sense.

But just because we can't explain it, doesn't mean it isn't true. In fact, it *is* true. And we're awfully glad it is.

Aren't you?

Note

1. C. S. Lewis, *The Four Loves* (New York: Harcourt, Brace & Co, 1960), p. 61.

THE GIFT OF INTELLIGENCE

Before Otto Octavius became a villain, he was a top-notch research scientist, specializing in atomic radiation and nuclear energy. He was, perhaps, even smarter than a rocket scientist. He was a brilliant thinker, but he knew the proper use of intelligence.

"Intelligence is a gift," Octavius told Peter Parker, "and you use it for the good of mankind."

Some of us have been better endowed with the gift of intelligence than others. Neither of your humble authors claims to be the sharpest knife in the drawer. Yet it does not matter how much or how little intelligence we have been given; we are to use what we have for others, not just ourselves.

That goes for any gift we have been given. The apostle Paul gave us a list of some of the gifts that are given by God to His followers. We can find his list in Romans 12:6-8 and in 1 Corinthians 12:8-11. They include:

- Preaching
- Being helpful
- Teaching
- Encouraging words
- Leadership
- Giving aid to those in distress
- Working with the disadvantaged
- Wise counsel
- Clear understanding
- Simple trust

- Healing the sick
- Miraculous acts
- Proclamation
- Distinguishing between spirits (*THE MESSAGE*)

We read that God decides who gets which gift and in what amount. So the first thing we need to understand about these gifts is that we cannot brag about which ones we have, or how much of them we have been given. We did not earn these—that is why they are called "gifts." If you have the gift of doing the miraculous, that does not mean you are better (or worse) than someone who is gifted in being helpful. Spiritual gifts are handed out by God in His way and in His measure.

The second thing to note about spiritual gifts is that we do not receive them to use for our own benefit. Remember what Otto Octavius says: "Intelligence is a gift, and you use it for the good of mankind."

The spiritual gifts we receive are to be used for the expansion of the kingdom of God. Paul wrote to the church at Rome these words about using their spiritual gifts:

> If you preach, just preach God's Message, nothing else; if you help, just help, don't take over; if you teach, stick to your teaching; if you give encouraging guidance, be careful that you don't get bossy; if you're put in charge, don't manipulate; if you're called to give aid to people in distress, keep your eyes open and be quick to respond; if you work with the disadvantaged, don't let yourself get irritated with them or depressed by them (Romans 12:6-8, *THE MESSAGE*).

Spiritual gifts, just like Octavius's gift of intelligence, are to be used for the good of others. When used in the wrong way and for the wrong reasons, gifts can become dangerous weapons: dangerous to others and ourselves.

Doc Ock uses the gift of intelligence for his own evil purposes. He wounds many others by his actions and ends up at the bottom of a river because of his greed. Just before he dies, though, he cries, "I will not die a monster!" He uses his gift one last time to destroy the ball of atomic energy threatening to destroy the city. At the end, he once again uses what was given to him for the good of mankind.

You have been given gifts by God, gifts unique to you. Two questions need to be answered:

    1. What are your unique gifts?
    2. Are you using them for the good of others?

To answer the first question, ask your pastor or youth leader if they have a test or guide that can show you what your gifts are. There are a number of excellent resources available for this, and most churches have access to one or more for you to use.

Once you have identified your gifts, it is time to get to work.

The best place to start is in prayer. Thank God for the gifts He has given you. (Remember, these are *gifts*. You did not earn them, and you cannot swap them for something else.) Ask God to open doors for you to use these spiritual gifts in a way that will help others. Working alongside the Creator is the most fun you can have. And as you put your specially given abilities to work in your faith community, you will be filling a gap that only you, with your unique gifts, can fill.

THE SMART ARMS OF SIN

Inventors like Dr. Otto Octavius are extremely creative. They can see things that don't exist—yet—and bring them to life. They come up with solutions to problems and create things that make our lives better.

That is just what Otto Octavius intends to do: He wants to create a new form of renewable energy to better everyone's lives. In order to manipulate the radioactive material used to create this energy field, Octavius develops a set of "smart arms." These arms are connected to his brain so that he can control them with his thoughts. Remember, he intends to use his thoughts—his intelligence—for the good of others.

"Doctor," asks a reporter witnessing the unveiling of the smart arms, "if the artificial intelligence in the arms is as advanced as you suggest, wouldn't that make you vulnerable to them?"

"How right you are," replies Otto. "Which is why I developed this inhibitor chip to protect my higher brain function. It means I maintain control of the arms, instead of them controlling me."

But something goes wrong—terribly wrong. A spike in the energy field shorts out the inhibitor chip. The collapsing energy field sets off a catastrophic accident that ends with Otto's wife, Rosie, dead, and the smart arms permanently fused to Octavius. No longer do the doctor's thoughts control the arms; the arms control Otto's thoughts. Thus is born the evil Doctor Octopus ("Doc Ock" to his friends).

Okay, so all this is science fiction. No one really has a set of smart arms controlling their thoughts, right? Right. But we often feel that something else is controlling us. Have you ever done something that was totally out of character for you? Or maybe you set off to say something encouraging but ended up harming another person with your words. Where is that inhibitor chip when we need it?

The apostle Paul asked the same question. He also felt out of control at times. He ended up doing wrong when he set out to do right, and said that he was helpless to stop doing what he knew he shouldn't. He wrote to the Christians in Rome and told them just how he felt:

> I can will it, but I can't do it. I decide to do good, but I don't really do it. I decide not to do bad, but then I do it anyway. My decisions, such as they are, don't result in actions. Something has gone wrong deep within me and gets the better of me every time (Romans 7:18-20, *THE MESSAGE*).

It sounds as if the smart arms of sin had taken control of Paul. Deep inside, he said, there was something wrong. He made up his mind to act one way, but his body reacted in a different way.

> It happens so regularly that it's predictable. The moment I decide to do good, sin is there to trip me up. I truly delight in God's commands, but it's pretty obvious that not all of me joins in that delight. Parts of me covertly rebel, and just when I least expect it, they take charge. I've tried everything, and nothing helps. I'm at the end of my rope. Is there no one who can do anything for me? (Romans 7:21-24, *THE MESSAGE*).

Paul was describing what happens when the inhibitor chip goes haywire. Octavius isn't in control of the arms any longer;

they are in charge of him: "Parts of me covertly rebel, and just when I least expect it, they take charge."

After the energy field explodes, destroying his lab and all of his equipment, Octavius returns with the four smart arms permanently attached to him and controlling his actions. He hears "something . . . in my head . . . something talking." This "something" tells him to rebuild the energy field and steal the money to make it happen. At first Otto rejects that idea. "I'm not a criminal," he says.

But the arms intercede. They whisper in his ear. And Otto changes his tune. "That's right," he says. "The real crime would be to not finish what we started."

Without the inhibitor chip, it doesn't matter that he doesn't want to do more damage—he is no longer in charge. The smart arms have taken over his thoughts and his actions, just as sin had its way in Paul's life. Just as sin has its way in our lives.

Paul cried out in anguish, "Who will set me free from this body of death?" (Romans 7:24, *NASB*). He could have been referring to an ancient practice where if you were to accidentally kill someone, you were made to wear the dead body strapped to yours for three days. The "body of death" would begin to rot and stink, and you wanted nothing less than to be rid of it. In the same way, Paul recognized that his old self, the "pre-Christian" Paul, was still part of him. But it was a dead way of life, stinking and rotting just like a corpse.

Who, indeed, could set him free? Paul offered the answer in verse 25:

> The answer, thank God, is that Jesus Christ can and does. He acted to set things right in this life of contradictions where I want to serve God with all my heart and mind, but am pulled by the influence of sin to do something totally different (Romans 7:25, *THE MESSAGE*).

Jesus is our inhibitor chip. He keeps the smart arms of sin from being in control of us.

How should this look in our lives? Paul gave us an idea in the previous chapter of Romans:

> From now on, think of it this way: Sin speaks a dead language that means nothing to you. God speaks your mother-tongue, and you hang on every word. You are dead to sin, and alive to God. That's what Jesus did. That means you must not give sin a vote in the way you conduct your lives. Don't give it the time of day. Don't even run little errands associated with your old way of life (Romans 6:11, *THE MESSAGE*).

We are dead to sin—the smart arms no longer have control over us. We don't have to listen to what they say or do what they tell us to do. We are no longer slaves to the arms of sin. We are now living in freedom—free from the arms that held us down, and free to run in the abundance of life that God has for us.

THE POWER OF THE SUN
IN THE PALM OF MY HAND

Let's assume for a moment that Otto Octavius's experiments are going to work. Obviously, he's done some research, probably some initial experimentation, just to be able to work those super-cool smart arms. And he knows enough to put that Inhibitor Chip in there, right? So surely he's done this experiment tons of times, the one where he puts the "precious tridium" into that big claw that lights up.

You remember the scene, right? It's where we're first introduced to Otto's smart arms, with that great shot of them locking around his abdomen. So nifty.

Okay, so we're just going to assume that Otto has done this a thousand times already—he's just never done it for an audience of press people and his bosses. So he puts the tridium, which has to be crazy expensive, since there are only 25 pounds of it "on the whole planet" (you may point out the inconsistency in Otto proposing a "cheap" source of energy that relies on crazy-expensive tridium, but we're just going to file that knowledge away so we don't have to think about it, okay?) into the big claw, and the different parts of the claw light up and shoot the tridium with little beams of light.

Poof! There's suddenly a miniature sun! We have a successful fusion reaction, everyone, and it is so hot, it's cool. Now, the actual heat radiating from that sun has to be intense (1000 megawatts of surplus energy sounds like a whole lot), which is the whole purpose of Otto's smart arms in the first place. They're the only things that can withstand the heat of the fusion reaction, and they're as much an extension of him as his real arms; at one point he caresses the sun with the open pincer of one of his smart arms and marvels, "The power of the sun in the palm of my hand."

And then the experiment goes haywire and the claw starts sucking in all the metal stuff and there's a containment breach and everyone freaks out and Otto's inhibitor chip gets damaged and a new villain is created and Spider-Man shows up to save the day. Okay, right. We got that part.

But let's back up to the point before the experiment goes haywire. Because up until then, it is a success. It is Otto's hubris that causes it to go belly-up; he won't shut it down when it starts to get out of his control, and that's what allows it to get out of hand and cause all that damage. So it isn't the experiment's fault—it's Otto's.

The experiment was working. Everyone there was witnessing fusion, the power of the sun in the palm of Otto's hand, for real. There's an interesting line delivered by some random Oscorp guy, whispered to Harry Osborn, Norman's son, "This is a breakthrough beyond your father's dreams."

We limit ourselves so often in this life. We come up with our own devices. We formulate our own plans for the way our life will unfold. We structure ourselves quite literally to death, laying out our preconceived notions of how we'll live until the inevitable moment when we cease to.

But our vision is so small. In Ephesians 3:20, the apostle Paul made this point in what is almost an aside to his readers:

> Now to him who is able to do immeasurably more than all we ask or imagine, according to his power that is at work within us, to him be glory in the church and in Christ Jesus throughout all generations, for ever and ever! Amen.

He wasn't really trying to make a point; he was just praising God . . . but that didn't stop him from laying the "able to do immeasurably more than all we ask or imagine" on us.

God is so much bigger than us. And he has such bigger plans for us than we have for ourselves. Think of it like this: Oftentimes, we look at our lives as if surveying our surroundings by the light of a candle. In a concrete bunker.

There's an image to run with. Think of a concrete bunker, or any room with no windows. And the room is filled with all sorts of cool stuff—maybe money or Aztec gold or genetically modified spiders. Now, imagine yourself in the middle of that room, holding a single candle. What would you be able to see? Not much. Maybe you could move around to try to glimpse some definition, but by and large, you'd be hard-pressed to take a specific survey of the room with that one candle.

This is how we look at our lives. Our view is dim, so our overall vision is lacking.

Now imagine that same room, but this time with no roof, in the midday sun. That candle suddenly seems pretty pathetic and pointless, doesn't it? In fact, you may not even be able to see the light from it, because it's so drowned out by the intense light of the shining sun.

Here's an interesting factoid about the sun. Since the 1960s, there's been talk of stashing a bunch of solar panels in space that would beam unfiltered solar energy down to earth for clean, constantly renewable electricity. Why? Because, according to a report from the Pentagon's National Security Space Office, "A single kilometer-wide band of geosynchronous Earth orbit experiences enough solar flux in one year to nearly equal the amount of energy contained within all known recoverable conventional oil reserves on Earth today."[1]

That's some serious power.

But it pales in comparison to the power of God.

The truth is that, as Christians, we *do* have the power of the figurative sun in the metaphorical palms of our hands. We have God on our side, taking an active interest in our lives, seeking to guide us and direct us in the way we should live. Why, if we have a choice between the power of the sun or a shoddy little candle, would we toss away the solar light for something so much dimmer?

Well, if we get selfish and start to think we're in control of the whole game, as Otto did, we can wind up making a big mess out of our intentions. We can't see the whole picture—so we need to quit looking with our own eyes and give our lives over to God's purposes.

Note

1. Lara Farmer, "How to Harvest Solar Power? Beam It Down from Space!" CNN.com Technology, June 1, 2008. http://www.cnn.com/2008/TECH/science/05/30/space.solar/index.html (accessed January 2010).

SPIDER-MAN NO MORE

It's an up and down thing, this life. Times of great happiness are often followed by times of deep sadness. And things we count on don't always pan out the way we thought they would.

Certainly true for Peter. Or Spider-Man, rather. He's in the middle of battling Doctor Octopus in the bank, and suddenly his webbing fails him. Later, he finds out that Mary Jane is engaged to young Astronaut Jameson and, during a therapeutic swing through the city, the webbing fails him again. He plummets to the earth like a rock, slamming first into the edge of a dumpster, then facedown in a puddle. Ick.

He pulls off his mask to reveal possibly the worst case of bedhead ever, and tries to spew some more webbing. No dice. "Why's this happening to me?" he wonders aloud. Curious, he wanders over to a nearby wall and begins his standard ascent. Halfway up, his powers fail him *again*, and he begins to slide down the wall. Ah, but then his powers kick back in, but only for a moment, and, like a car sputtering as it runs out of gas, Peter eventually succumbs to his predicament, landing with a thud on the alley floor, his tank on empty.

Good thing his super-strength hasn't failed him, or those falls would've been a lot worse, huh?

Oh, yeah . . . his spider-bite-enhanced vision is messing up too, to the point where even the words "Spidey and Ock Rob Bank" emblazoned in thousand-point font on the front page of the *Daily Bugle* become blurry.

So what's a superhero to do when the very things that make him super begin to go away? Visit the doctor, duh. But not just any doctor—Peter decides to see a physician who practices wearing the standard white lab coat over a tie-dyed t-shirt. Sweet.

The doc (not Ock) looks him over and proclaims, "It's all in your mind." He asks if Peter's been having bad dreams or anything, so Peter leaps on the opportunity to get a full-blooded physician's opinion on the whole superpower-loss thing.

"I have a dream," Peter tentatively says, "where *I'm* Spider-Man." And then he unloads on the poor doc, telling him how all his superpowers have gone out, how he climbs walls—in his dream—and then falls. Stuff like that. In fact, it isn't even his dream; it's his friend's dream. Yeah, that's right. His friend's.

The doctor puts aside the tongue depressor and takes a seat next to Peter on the examination table. Time for a little psychoanalysis. "Why does your friend climb these walls?" he asks. "Who is he?"

The diagnosis for us, the viewers: Peter is conflicted. He doesn't know who he is. He's trying to be Spider-Man *and* Peter Parker at the same time, and it's messing with his superhero mojo.

"Maybe you're not supposed to be Spider-Man climbing those walls," the doc tells him. "You always have a choice, Peter."

What's a superhero to do? Peter thinks about it, this choice. He can't let go of his love for Mary Jane enough to be Spider-Man. He's tired of the duality of his nature. He wants his life back, and he makes the decision: He is Spider-Man no more. And he demonstrates by chucking his Spidey outfit into a back alley garbage can.

As a conflicted individual, Peter can find no stability. Sometimes his Spider-Man-ness shows up while he's Peter; more dangerously, sometimes his Peter Parker-ness shows up while he's Spider-Man (leading to a lack of webbing at crucial apexes of city-wide swing sessions).

Sometimes we feel unaware of who we are, maybe when life presents us with a difficult choice that we cannot even begin to make. Occasionally, life hammers us over the head so hard that we feel like we lose our ability to cope—whatever superpowers we utilize to make it through the day are gone. One minute, we're soaring through the air, effortlessly—and the next, whatever we were soaring on has been yanked out from under us and we are now rapidly heading downward for a date with a dumpster.

What can we do in such situations? What can we do when life smacks us across the face with trials galore? We can turn to the advice we find in James 1:2-8:

> Consider it pure joy, my brothers, whenever you face trials of many kinds, because you know that the testing of your faith develops perseverance. Perseverance must finish its work so that you may be mature and complete, not lacking anything. If any of you lacks wisdom, he should ask God, who gives generously to all without finding fault, and it will be given to him. But when he asks, he must believe and not doubt, because he who doubts is like a wave of the sea, blown and tossed by the wind. That man should not think he will receive anything from the Lord; he is a double-minded man, unstable in all he does.

When life hits you over the head with trouble—and believe me, it will—you have a couple of options. You can fret and worry and get all in a huff about it. Or you can take it to God, ask Him for wisdom, listen and then do what He says. We can have confidence, according to this passage in James, that when we ask God for help in the midst of our trials, He'll give it to us.

But if we ask God half-heartedly, then we get into a whole doubt thing, and doubt things only make us unstable. Doubting makes us double-minded, always unsure that we're doing the right thing, wondering if we should have made the *other* choice, if the other wasn't really the *right* one. So we switch to that other choice, thinking that it must be the right choice, but then it doesn't feel right, and now the *first* choice sounds like it might've been the right choice all along.

Back and forth, back and forth, like a wave of the sea, blown and tossed by the wind. Being double-minded is exhausting and painful, as Peter Parker finds out firsthand.

But once he rises up in the fullness of his destiny, once he again determines to live up to his Uncle Ben's credo, "with great power comes great responsibility," Peter is no longer unstable. Instead, he becomes a hero once again.

It can be the same in our own lives. Instead of being double-minded, let's go back to the root of what we know—let's go back to the Bible. Go back to God. Go back.

Let us all be double-minded no more.

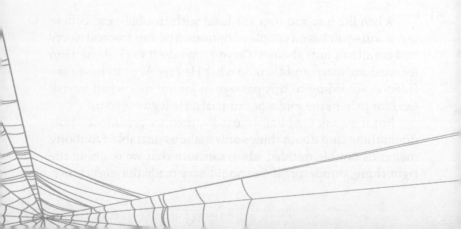

A HERO IN ALL OF US

Spider-Man 2 deals with the duality of mankind—our ability to be bad or good, based on the choices we make: either to stand up to the inevitable evil that we encounter in this world or to let it rage unchecked.

The filmmakers illustrate this in a long scene between Peter and Aunt May. She's being forced out of her home for monetary reasons, and does a whole lot of packing while Peter just stands there. She has hired the nine-year-old boy from across the street to help with the task (something he does much better than Peter), and they've been discussing the curious lack of Spider-Man in the city. What's he been up to?

Peter has been experiencing doubts about his calling to be super, and has chucked his Spidey suit in the trash. But now the crime rate in the city is appallingly high—where in the world is Spider-Man? Henry, the neighbor kid, asks Peter this very question, and Peter lamely replies that Spider-Man quit to try other things.

Fortunately, Henry doesn't press the issue with a well-placed "*what* other things?" Instead, his hopeful response is just: "He'll be back, right?"

"I don't know."

Peter really doesn't know. His life has been crazy, with all the trying to be a college student, a photographer and a superhero.

And make no mistake: Spider-Man is a hero. But while it's easy to focus on the cool stuff—the sticking to walls, the webbing that shoots from his wrists, the super strength, the ability to take a punch that would send the rest of us to the ER—Aunt May rightfully points out that those things aren't what make Spidey a hero.

Nope. As Aunt May puts it, heroes are "courageous, self-sacrificing people, setting examples for all of us." According to her, heroes are people who tell the rest of us "to hold on one second longer."

Then Aunt May holds forth on heroes in everyday life, and delivers what may be the most truth-packed line in the entire *Spider-Man* series: "I believe there's a hero in all of us." This theoretical hero "keeps us honest, gives us strength, makes us noble and finally allows us to die with pride."

Ah, but there's a hitch that comes with being a hero—because heroism inevitably involves self-sacrifice, giving up something (or someone) we really care for in order to serve the greater good.

Can *you* be a hero? Yes! Maybe not in the sense that Aunt May means, when she says that "there's a hero in all of us." Taken one way, that can be a remarkably humanistic statement, one that propagates the notion that we are all inherently good. The apostle Paul wrote in Romans 8 that we all have a sinful nature that does its best to waylay our good intentions ("the sinful mind is hostile to God. It does not submit to God's law, nor can it do so . . . those controlled by the sinful nature cannot please God" [vv. 7-8]). Our sinful minds are the antithesis of a "hero in all of us."

But Paul then wrote this, in the very next verse: "You, however, are controlled not by the sinful nature but by the Spirit, if the Spirit of God lives in you" (v. 9). There you go! You can shake off that sinful nature with God's help. And the heroism part comes later on, in Romans 8:12-17:

> Therefore, brothers, we have an obligation—but it is not to the sinful nature, to live according to it. For if you live

according to the sinful nature, you will die; but if by the Spirit you put to death the misdeeds of the body, you will live, because those who are led by the Spirit of God are sons of God. For you did not receive a spirit that makes you a slave again to fear, but you received the Spirit of sonship. And by him we cry, "Abba, Father." The Spirit himself testifies with our spirit that we are God's children. Now if we are children, then we are heirs—heirs of God and co-heirs with Christ, if indeed we share in his sufferings in order that we may also share in his glory.

Think of that. "We share in his sufferings in order that we may also share in his glory." It's the very idea of self-sacrifice as a necessary part of heroism, isn't it?

So there is a hero in all of us—if we have given up our sinful nature and become sons of God, that is. We all have the capacity to be nice to each other, yes, and the ability to show compassion to our fellow man. But if we want to be truly heroic, we have to give up our sinful nature and all that entails—all our own selfish pursuits—and adhere to Romans 6:6-7: "For we know that our old self was crucified with him so that the body of sin might be done away with, that we should no longer be slaves to sin—because anyone who has died has been freed from sin."

Letting go of our old selves is the first step to true heroism—making God's priorities our own. And once we start down that road, we can truly give way to the "hero in all of us."

I WAS RESPONSIBLE

What is the hardest thing for Spider-Man to do? Rescuing Aunt May from the side of the building where Doc Ock has left her hanging? Stopping a runaway commuter train before it plunged off the tracks? Destroying the source of power created from tridium by Doc Ock and saving the whole city?

The hardest task faced by Spider-Man—harder even than holding a metal wall that would have crushed Mary Jane ("This is really heavy," says Spidey)—shows up while he is sitting in the dining room of Aunt May's house. Shortly after Peter and Aunt May return from visiting Uncle Ben's grave, after hearing Aunt May once again grieve over the loss of her husband, Peter knows that he can no longer keep the truth about Uncle Ben's death a secret.

"You wanted to take the subway," Aunt May recalls, "and he wanted to drive you. If only I had stopped him, we'd all three of us be having tea together."

For some time now, Peter has let Aunt May think that he went where he said he was going the night Uncle Ben was killed. For all Aunt May knows, Peter did go to the library that night to do his homework. But Peter can no longer hold onto his secret. He is visibly shaken. He stares at the table, at the teacups, mustering the courage to begin his confession. He starts with two simple but very powerful words:

"I'm responsible."

How often do we fight these words? Rather than confess that something was our fault, we point the blame just about anywhere else. For example:

"I didn't do it."

"It was an accident."

"I was just kidding."

To admit something was my doing—to say that it was my fault, that I am responsible—is the only way I can begin to get free of the weight of guilt I carry.

But why should I, or Peter Parker, confess? If Aunt May thinks it was her fault, why not just let it stay that way? Is confession really necessary?

In a word, yes. Read what the prophet Isaiah wrote:

> But your iniquities have separated you from your God;
> and your sins have hidden His face from you, so that
> He will not hear (Isaiah 59:2, *NKJV*).

Wow. I always want the communication channel open between God and me. If I don't confess my sins, it seems that my relationship with my heavenly Father is going to suffer.

John, one of Jesus' closest followers, also wrote about confession of sins: "If we say that we have no sin, we deceive ourselves, and the truth is not in us" (1 John 1:8, *NKJV*). *THE MESSAGE* renders the same verse like this: "If we claim that we're free of sin, we're only fooling ourselves. A claim like that is errant nonsense." If I keep my sin closed up inside of me, I am fooling myself. But if I confess, "He is faithful and just to forgive us our sins and to cleanse us from all unrighteousness" (1 John 1:9, *NKJV*).

Before we look further at what confession is and how to properly confess our sins, let's look at what confession is *not*. Confession is not speculation ("If I did something wrong, I'm sorry"). It's not admitting to a mistake (2 + 2 = 5 is a mistake; God forgives sin, not mistakes). It's not just getting something off of your chest. Confession is not to be done lightly—after all, by confessing we are asking to be forgiven by God. And forgiveness cost God His only Son, Jesus.

So what *is* confession?

The Greek word for "confess" is *homologeo*, which means "to say the same thing." In essence, confession is agreeing with God about our actions. It is to say the same thing God says about what we have done: If He considers our action sinful, we need to agree and confess that sin. We must start by calling sin what it is—not a mistake, a lapse of judgment, a slip-up. It's sin, plain and simple.

David sinned with Bathsheba, who was not his wife. He compounded the sin by having her husband murdered. Once he was confronted with his actions, he didn't mince words. He came before God and said:

> For I acknowledge my transgressions, and my sin is always before me. Against You, and You only have I sinned, and done this evil in Your sight—that you may be found just when You speak (Psalm 51:3-4, *NKJV*).

It's not easy to confess sin. Peter would rather be swinging through the city in pursuit of bad guys than sitting in the dining room with Aunt May, telling her that it was because of his actions that she is a widow. But he *does* confess, and in the right manner. He tells the whole story and doesn't make excuses. He confesses his actions ("The thief was running toward me," says Peter, "and I could have stopped him") as well as his motives ("But I wanted revenge"). We don't know what Peter is hoping for when he makes this confession, but we do see Aunt May's response: She pulls her hand away from Peter and goes upstairs, leaving him alone at the table.

The immediate effect of our confession may be the same. We may be shunned or rejected by those to whom we admit our sins. Even so, we must go forward with it.

But to whom do we confess our sins? In every case, to God. It's not like we are going to surprise Him with our admission of sin; He knows it already. But God is the one to whom we must go because our sin cost Him the most.

If our sin was only something we did within ourselves—unprovoked anger, lust, pride, laziness—then confessing these sins to God and asking Him to help us overcome them may be where our confession begins and ends. But if our sin has affected another person, we need to ask forgiveness from the one we have hurt even before we ask for God's forgiveness. This is very important, so important that Jesus told us not even to enter a worship service until we make things right with others:

> This is how I want you to conduct yourself in these matters. If you enter your place of worship and, about to make an offering, you suddenly remember a grudge a friend has against you, abandon your offering, leave immediately, and go to this friend and make things right. Then and only then, come back and work things out with God (Matthew 5:23-24, *THE MESSAGE*).

We must be careful not to "confess" to someone who was not involved in our situation. It is easier to share our sin with a close friend, someone we know will likely not reject us. That may make us feel better, but if we did not sin against that friend, our confession is in vain. We must confess to those we hurt by our sin.

Asking for forgiveness is very hard, but the reward is great. Once we are forgiven, we can, in a way, recover our superpowers. In James we read, "Make this your common practice: Confess your sins to each other and pray for each other so that you can live together whole and healed" (5:16, *THE MESSAGE*).

Peter Parker's confession is the first step toward regaining his ability to spin webs—to once again become who he is meant to be: Spider-Man. Our confession is a continual step in becoming who *we* are meant to be: people who live glorious lives in pursuit of God.

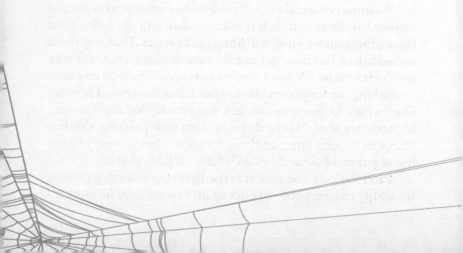

EVEN SUPERHEROES
NEED HELP

John Donne famously wrote, many, many years ago (it was in 1623, if you must know) that "no man is an island, entire of itself." This English poet saw, even 400 years ago, that a life lived completely alone is a dull thing.

There is no historical record as to whether Donne said, "I'm getting married in a church," but Mary Jane says it to Peter early on in *Spider-Man 2*. He had been sure that she would get married on a hilltop, but no, she flatly corrects him. A church it is.

And what a church! At the end of the movie, we see the church that Mary Jane meant, a giant, ornamental cathedral, spires reaching to the skies. The architecture itself is a cheery celebration of joy.

Ah, but within the ornate décor, Mary Jane's lonesome expression stands as a perfect counterpoint to the opulence around her. Yes, she's a beautiful bride, but she's begun to realize that she's marrying the wrong man (his astronaut status notwithstanding).

Cut to the wedding—a lavish, extravagant affair with flowers all over the place . . . and a jilted groom, who is handed a note by, one assumes, Mary Jane's friend or maid of honor or someone like that.

Never one for subtlety, Sam Raimi, the film's director, then treats us to a shot of Mary Jane running through a sun-dappled park, trees in full bloom, white doves fluttering behind her, the fountain joyously erupting, all shot in gauzy hues that lend the whole proceedings an aura of heavenly light. MJ is taking her life into her own hands! Who cares that she now knows Peter is Spider-Man? Or that he'd told her they can't be together? Or that he views rejecting her as a means of protecting her? She's smiling, following her own heart.

And where is she running? She's headed to Peter's apartment, where he is morosely looking out the window, his back to the open door (why is it open, exactly?). He notices her presence and she tells him, "I had to do what I had to do."

Much speechifying follows, where she points out to him that it's not up to him to decide how she should handle her heart. If she wants to be with him and sign up for all the dangers that connotes, then that's her right.

But what she says in the midst of that cuts to the core of everything that sucks about being a superhero: "Isn't it about time somebody saved your life?"

It's the catch-22 of superhero-dom. Sure, you do a lot of good for people and, you know, save the world again and again . . . but you do it all alone. You don't have anyone to confide in, anyone to share your troubles with, anyone to give you a hand when you really need it.

And make no mistake, you'll need it. Peter says as much toward the end of *Spider-Man 3*, when he's rushing off to take care of Sandman and Venom and pleads with his friend Harry Osborn for help. He says it in *Spider-Man 2*, when faced with the prospect of his own demise at the hands of a vengeful Harry, when he tells his friend, "There are bigger things here at stake than you and me."

Even superheroes need help. And if *superheroes* need it, you better believe we mere mortals need it. Except here in this life, we don't just call it "help"; we call it "accountability."

The often-quoted biblical passage for this concept comes from Proverbs 27:17, which says, "As iron sharpens iron, so one man sharpens another." Peter saves Mary Jane from the clutches of the Green Goblin and from Doctor Octopus, and now it's time for Mary Jane to save Peter from a life of loneliness, despair and pent-up emotion.

We see the idea of accountability and assistance in the actions of Jesus, who did not operate in isolation. He had the 12 disciples with Him, and whenever He sent them on special tasks, He sent them out in pairs, never alone (see Matthew 21:1; Mark 6:7; Mark 11:1; Luke 10:1). During the apostle Paul's missionary journeys, he always traveled with someone else and never went out on his own.

This concept of accountability can also be found in the Old Testament, in the story of Nehemiah and the rebuilding of the wall around Jerusalem. The wall had been ransacked and torn down by Israel's enemies, and Nehemiah led the effort to get it back up. The entire book of Nehemiah is about this task, and chapter 3 lists each person that participated in the rebuilding process and which part of the wall they rebuilt. It's a classic example of people helping each other out to achieve an objective greater than themselves.

While most of us will never take on the colossal job of rebuilding a wall around an entire city, we all undertake the no-less-colossal job of living this life. And though we might get through it okay on our own, it is so much more sharp, diverse, rich and rewarding if we have at least one other person involved— and not just someone to help us, but someone we can help, too. Someone who sharpens us and who we, in turn, sharpen.

The time has come to get off our own personal islands. The time has come to get involved in other people's lives, and to invite other people to get involved in ours. If we could get some accountability like that? That'd be super.

PART THREE

SPIDER-MAN 3 (2007)

INT. PETER'S APARTMENT - NIGHT*

PETER, in his SPIDER-MAN SUIT, no mask, sits on the
edge of his bed, tense, ready. His gaze is intent on
the POLICE SCANNER sitting on his nightstand.

The scanner squawks intermittently, letting Peter in on
the criminal goings-on throughout the city. He doesn't
respond to any of them, though. He is listening for one
thing and one thing only: news of Flint Marko.

He is ready to exact his super revenge.

CUT TO:
INT. PETER'S APARTMENT - LATER

Peter now stands, his enthusiasm wavering. He's
tired, leaning against the doorpost, willing his eyes
to stay open. He is losing the fight.

In the background, the scanner still squawks, still
steering clear of the news Peter craves.

DISSOLVE TO:
INT. PETER'S APARTMENT - LATER

Peter is now lying on the bed, asleep, the scanner
still squawking.

Peter's sleep is troubled. Restless. We zoom in
on him from above as THUNDER AND LIGHTNING begin
outside. Suddenly, Peter jumps in his sleep, and as
he jumps, we ...

FLASH CUT TO:
EXT. SIDEWALK - CONTINUOUS (B/W)

Uncle Ben, sitting in his car.

Flint Marko, tapping on the window of the car, star-
tling Uncle Ben.

BACK TO:
INT. PETER'S APARTMENT - CONTINUOUS

We are low to the ground, from the POV of the SYMBIOTE,
the black substance that attached itself to Peter's
scooter. The view is distorted, and we can hear the
alien's thrum as if it came from our own lips.

We're scanning, scanning the room. We see Peter on the
bed; he startles awake. Seeing nothing, he goes back
to sleep.

Slowly, we glide along the floor, strewn with clothes
and other detritus. We glide up to the bed and along
the blankets, up to Peter's costumed hand.

CUT TO:

Peter lying on the bed, asleep. On the far wall
behind him, we see a silhouette, a strange shape made
up of sentient strands of goo. The strands form into
a rudimentary hand, or claw.

The claw leans in and seemingly attacks Peter.

Peter jumps, but remains asleep.

FLASH CUT TO:
EXT. SIDEWALK - CONTINUOUS (B/W)

Uncle Ben, lying on the sidewalk, trying to evade a captor.

BACK TO:
INT. PETER'S APARTMENT - CONTINUOUS

The strands of black goo are now making their way up
Peter's hand, fusing themselves to his Spider-Man suit.

FLASH CUT TO:
EXT. SIDEWALK - CONTINUOUS (B/W)

Uncle Ben, still trying to get away.

Flint Marko holds a gun on him. He shoots.

Uncle Ben takes the shot.
BACK TO:

INT. PETER'S APARTMENT - CONTINUOUS

Peter jumps again, but remains asleep. The symbiote
continues attaching itself, working its way up
Peter's suit. It is fusing with his other hand now.
Now it's working its way down the legs of the suit.

FLASH CUT TO:
INT. ABANDONED WAREHOUSE - NIGHT (B/W)

We flash back to Peter, in the first film, and his
confrontation with the car thief:

                         THIEF
                Just give me a chance!

                         PETER
                  What about my uncle?
            Did you give him a chance? Did you?

The thief goes out the window.

He's lying on the docks below, dead.

BACK TO:
INT. PETER'S APARTMENT - CONTINUOUS

The symbiote makes its way up Peter's chest, re-creating the famous Spider-Man icon in the process. Up his neck. The strands reach out from all directions to cover his face.

The strands reach into his mouth, his eyes, his nose, and as they do, Peter wakes with a start, eyes wide. But it is too late.

We zoom in on Peter's widening eye as he is completely covered by the strands.

The bonding is complete. Peter now has a means to quench his thirst for revenge.

"I'M NOT A BAD PERSON"

We, Adam and Jeff, have a joint confession to make. Ready? Here goes:

We're bad people.

We hope this hasn't damaged our relationship with you. We feel it shouldn't, because, honestly? So are you.

You're a bad person.

Wait! Don't shut the book in exasperation. We have a reason to say what we're saying. But before we do, let's look at the introduction of Flint Marko's character in *Spider-Man 3*.

The first time we see Flint Marko, he's on the run. He has escaped from prison, and the cops are hard on his tail. He darts down an alleyway and we see him in silhouette, narrowly evading the probing searchlight of a passing police cruiser. He hides out long enough to escape the probing beam and heads to the fire escape to climb the ladder.

Once on the fire escape, Flint gently opens a window and steps into his daughter, Penny's, bedroom. She lies on the bed, sleeping like the little angel she is, oxygen tubes in her nose, the tank supplying them nearby. Flint looks at her for a long while, considering, taking her in. Then he reaches into his prison uniform and produces a thick packet of mail: letters he'd written to Penny that had been sent back, rejected by his wife, Penny's mother. Carefully, he slides them under her pillow.

An outfit change and a torn hunk of bread later, we find our anti-hero in the kitchen, being discovered by his long-suffering wife. She tells him that he can't hide there in their apartment, and Flint Marko finally utters his first line of the entire picture: "I'm just here to see my daughter."

Turns out Flint Marko is a loving father, who just happens to show his love in inappropriate ways: by stealing money to heal her, then getting thrown in the slammer for it.

But a little thing like jail (or a particle accelerator) isn't enough to keep Flint from his beloved Penny—and so here he is, an escaped convict, hoping to at least see his little girl before going back on the run. His wife points as much out, tacking on the wounding words, "You're nothing but a common thief."

Their conversation devolves into a minor argument, until both Flint and his wife hear the creak of a door. Penny is standing in the doorway to her bedroom, supporting herself on a crutch. She has overheard the whole thing.

It's okay, though. Flint kneels down to talk to her, and she gives him a locket, with a picture of herself inside, as a reminder of her love. He promises that he'll do whatever it takes to make her healthy again, but the sound of sirens in the background cuts the reunion short. It's time for Flint to leave, and his wife orders him to get out.

Flint clutches the locket, walks to the window (he can't go out the front door, silly—the cops are out there!) and opens it. He climbs out, then pauses on the landing of the fire escape to think for a moment. He knows he needs to say something. He may not get a chance to speak to his wife and child again. What words will he use?

"I'm not a bad person. I've just had bad luck."

And . . . scene.

It's a heartfelt moment, intended to establish Flint Marko as essentially a decent human being who has been forced by life to make a bunch of bad choices in order to survive. And in a practical way, that makes sense: Flint doesn't have bad motives in his heart—he isn't evil for the sake of being evil. He isn't stealing to feed his own greed. He isn't bent on world domination or, like his eventual partner, Venom, spurred on by an insatiable thirst for revenge.

He's just trying to make his daughter better. Who can have a problem with that?

But in a spiritual sense, Flint's words couldn't be less true. Because in a spiritual sense, despite his good heart, he *is* a bad person.

So are we. So are you.

We're *all* bad people. The Bible says as much in Romans 3. Check this out, in verses 19-24:

> Now we know that whatever the law [that's the Mosaic law, found in the Old Testament] says, it says to those who are under the law, so that every mouth may be silenced and the whole world held accountable to God. Therefore no one will be declared righteous in his sight by observing the law; rather, through the law we become conscious of sin.
>
> But now righteousness from God, apart from law, has been made known, to which the Law and the Prophets testify. This righteousness from God comes through faith in Jesus Christ to all who believe. There is no difference, for all have sinned and fall short of the glory of God, and are justified freely by his grace through the redemption that came by Christ Jesus.

Verse 23, the one that says, "for all have sinned and fall short of the glory of God," tends to be one of the most quoted texts from the New Testament. But look at all the stuff that goes before it: Before Jesus died, we all tried our hardest to become good people, but we couldn't do it—all we did was become aware that we were bad.

So then Jesus came and died for our sins, and then rose again, and now *all* of us, because we've all sinned and come up short when it comes to the glory of God, are able to be justified. When we accept the sacrifice of Jesus, we become "good" people. No, we are not suddenly sin-proof, but we are now on God's good side, which is the best place to be.

So Flint has it wrong—he *is* a bad person, who will eventually go through a pretty staggering journey toward healing his hurts. Unfortunately, he never gets "justified freely by [God's] grace through the redemption that came by Christ Jesus."

Whether you've had a life of good luck or bad luck, you are a person in need of God's grace. Just like Flint Marko. Just like all of us.

THE ROOT OF BITTERNESS

He doesn't see it coming.

Peter and MJ are enjoying a romantic moment together, resting in a web spun between two trees in Central Park, watching falling stars. One of those "stars" falls all the way to earth, landing near Peter's scooter. (And for some reason, Peter's Spidey sense does not detect the crash landing of a meteorite. Is he so consumed by his love for MJ that he cannot detect danger?)

A slimy black substance crawls out of the crater made by the meteorite and grabs on to the back of the departing scooter. It somehow makes its way into Peter's apartment and waits. And waits. And waits.

Then comes the day when Peter learns that escaped convict Flint Marko is the man who shot and killed Uncle Ben. That night, Peter lies in bed, wracked with images of his uncle gunned down by Marko. And the symbiote sees its chance. As Peter's bitterness and hatred toward Marko grow, the symbiote latches onto him. Its black fibers crawl over his legs, his hand, his face. The next thing Peter knows, he is outside on the ledge, covered in a new black Spider-Man suit. It feels good. It gives him greater powers. He is stronger. But the nature of the symbiote will destroy Peter.

What is a symbiote anyway? In the fictional world of Marvel Comics heroes, a symbiote is a living organism that must attach itself to some other living being in order to survive. Dr. Connors, examining the black substance brought to him by Peter, says it has the characteristics of a symbiote. He says, "Sometimes these things in nature, when they bind, they can be hard to unbind."

Once attached, the symbiote feeds off its host's emotions, especially adrenaline. Thus, the symbiote encourages the host to do wild and crazy things in order to get the adrenaline pumping. Spidey, upon seeing himself clad in the new black costume, stretches and twists, then does a back flip off of a skyscraper, happily screaming all the way down to the street below, where he fires off a web and swings through traffic. He takes greater risks in the black suit. He is bolder, more confident in his own powers.

And he uses the newfound powers to hunt down and kill Sandman, a.k.a. Flint Marko.

The "old" Spider-Man (or should we call him "Spidey Classic"?) didn't try to kill bad guys, but rather to catch and turn them over to the police. But black-suited Spidey does not pull his punch. He opens an underground water tank in order to wash Sandman away to his death. And he feels good doing it.

Have you ever felt like something has taken control of your emotions? You lash out in anger at a friend and then wonder why you did it. You shout something rude to someone without any real reason. You get angry at your parents and hold a grudge. Has a symbiote taken hold of you?

In the Bible we read about something similar to a symbiote. It is called the "root of bitterness" (Hebrews 12:5). Bitterness can occur when someone has wronged us. Of course, this happens every day. We get upset and offended by all kinds of things, big and little—and most of the time we are able to let it go, to forgive the offender right away. But sometimes we hold the offense close to us. We roll it over and over in our minds. Soon, the anger we are feeling has taken root and grown to a size that is much larger than the offence deserves. And you know what? The anger boiling inside makes us feel good—for a while. Because we are the "victim" of the wrong, we feel justified riding that angry feeling for as long as we can. It takes over our mind—we can't watch TV, read a book or carry on a conversation with someone without anger being front and center in our thoughts.

We like holding onto anger; bitter herbs taste sweet at first. Have you ever tried eating uncooked mustard greens? They have a slightly sweet taste when you first start chewing them. But when you swallow, look out. A bitter taste overwhelms your tongue and mouth, chasing away the sweetness. That is the way anger is: It may be sweet at first, but the longer we chew, the harsher it becomes. Bitterness grips us firmly and affects every area of our lives.

If bitterness is the root, what will the fruit of the tree be like? An apple tree has apple tree roots. It produces juicy apples, good to eat. But if the roots are bitter, the fruit of that tree will be bitter. In other words, if you allow anger to take root, all areas of your life will eventually taste bitter. The symbiote, once it binds to its host, is very hard to unbind.

So how do we get rid of bitterness and anger in our lives? The world offers two solutions: Hold the anger inside, and the poison of it will make you sick—both spiritually and physically. Or you can spew your anger to others and spread the poison around. Neither option is particularly appealing.

God offers a third option: Come before Him and confess what you have done. Agree with Him that you have held onto anger, which has grown into bitterness. Ask Him to help you become free from the black suit. In order to be set free from the bitterness, we need to forgive the one who made us angry in the first place. Forgiveness sets us, and the one who offended us, free.

Spider-Man feels good, at first, in the black suit, but soon it overwhelms him. It makes him act in ways that scare him. He is not in control of his actions or emotions. And it's not until he is back to the real Spider-Man that he is able to rescue Mary Jane and defeat his enemies.

Don't let anger and bitterness take root in your life. When you feel that pull toward bitterness, take it to God and let Him eradicate it. And for heaven's sake, don't do what Peter does—don't tuck it away in a suitcase in the back of the closet to pull out at an opportune moment. Instead, let it go. Forgive.

Truly forgive. Uproot the bitterness and plant forgiveness instead. You will love the fruit.

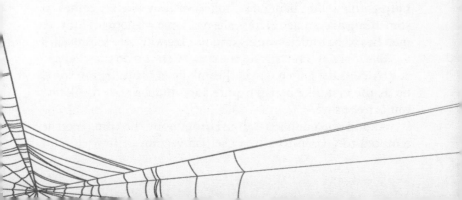

WIFE BEFORE HUSBAND

In *Spider-Man 3*, Peter runs smack into Aunt May's homespun wisdom a mere 15 minutes into the picture. His life is running along at a fantastic pace, something he tells us in voiceover narration as the movie opens. The city is in love with Spider-Man. He's acing his classes. And, most importantly, he's in love with the woman of his dreams: Mary Jane Watson.

MJ is doing well, too. Their relationship is blossoming, thanks to her forthrightness at the end of the previous film. Her acting career is taking off—she's appearing in a Broadway show, with her name on the marquee. And Peter is able to do what he had difficulty doing in the entire previous film: come to see her perform.

Yes, they are in love, and they're both giddy at it. Mary Jane just wants to sing for the rest of her life, with Peter in the front row to watch her . . . and Peter is on board with that, for sure.

He's so on board that he wakes up Aunt May in the middle of the night with a surprise visit, and a surprise announcement: He's going to ask Mary Jane to marry him. Aunt May is, naturally, thrilled. But, being a seasoned veteran when it comes to something as complex as love, she has some wisdom for him: "A man has to be understanding and put his wife before himself."

She looks at him, dead in the eyes. "Can you do that, Peter?"

He considers, then: "Yeah. I think I can," turning the "can" up at the end, like he isn't quite sure. But he sounds like he wants to be sure.

And in the end, he *is* sure. Throughout the film, Peter is tempted to give in to a more selfish version of himself, and though he does give in to some extent, he never goes completely all the way with it. Yes, he hurts Mary Jane by flaunting Gwen Stacy in front of her, and he lets the black suit, the symbiote, take control of him for a while. But he comes to his senses as the film closes and, as Harry teaches him, chooses to do what's right.

Peter chooses to put Mary Jane ahead of his own pride and, in a wonderful closing scene, comes to watch her sing, taking a position front and center—exactly what MJ requested at the beginning of the film. It's a nice little reminder of doing the right thing, putting his (hopefully soon-to-be) wife before himself.

What does that have to do with us, here on a spiritual level? What's the point of putting others before ourselves? There's a lot of truth to the idea that a husband must put his wife before himself (and that a wife should put her husband before herself, as long as we're talking about it). But is it possible that the Bible's prescription for husbands and wives—put the other before yourself—has a broader spiritual application? Say, for those of us who aren't married?

Yes. For starters, it really is a better way to live: putting others first, rather than making yourself the center of your existence. When you put yourself first, you're putting the focus on the wrong thing—your very flawed person. And when you focus solely on yourself, you're only going to be, eventually, disappointed. It's much better to make others your focus, and in so doing, you'll wind up taking care of yourself along the way.

Second, and most importantly, we are to put others before ourselves because *that's what Jesus did for us*. Jesus willingly put us—the entire world—before Himself, when He went to the cross.

We see this selflessness evident in God's view toward humanity in the very famous passage of Scripture found in John 3:16-17:

> For God so loved the world that he gave his one and only
> Son, that whoever believes in him shall not perish but

have eternal life. For God did not send his Son into the world to condemn the world, but to save the world through him.

God put us before Himself. He did the hardest thing anyone has ever done when He sent Jesus to the world to die an unjust death at the hands of unjust people in order to redeem the very people—us—who killed Him. It wasn't fair, but it was the plan. Jesus had every right, according to our natural human logic, to fight against the false charges that were leveled against Him (see Matthew 26:59-68) . . . but He didn't. Instead, He willingly took on the task laid out for Him (see Matthew 26:36-44). That task was putting others—the whole human race—before Himself.

But notice this: It didn't set Jesus back. His life and legacy weren't ruined because He put others before Himself.

Instead, it was that very selfless act that became the hinge of history.

It was what made Jesus *Jesus*. His ministry on earth was phenomenal, and we've never seen anything like it since. But it was His death and resurrection that made Him more than a good man. It was His death and resurrection that made Him our *Savior*.

Jesus' selflessness changed the game. And when we put others before ourselves, when we prefer them over us, we are associating with the sacrifice of Jesus. We aren't becoming deities, not by any stretch of the imagination. But we are emulating Him—re-creating, on a small scale, the holiest, the bravest of all acts.

What better example can we follow?

RISE OF THE SANDMAN

Superheroes and supervillains always get the coolest abilities. We normal simpletons down here just live boring ol' lives, while those guys get some fantastical transformation that gives them cool powers that they use for good or for evil.

Us, your humble authors? We just wish we had the power to figure out how to set the clock on the microwave.

And there are *two* of us.

Still, in the comics and movies, superheroes always start off as regular folk like the rest of us, then undergo some crazy transformation to become something super.

Take, for example, the rise of the Sandman. On the run from the law, Flint Marko tries to find refuge in a big field. But the field isn't big enough, apparently, because he finds himself being chased by police officers and growling, snapping dogs.

Ah, but what's this? A chain-link fence! With razor wire on top of it! Surely no one but Flint can overcome this obstacle. He scrambles over the fence (but not before punching out one of those mean dogs), which is helpfully labeled with a chuckle-inducing sign: PARTICLE PHYSICS TEST FACILITY: KEEP OUT.

Just so you know.

Flint keeps on running and stumbles headlong into a big pit of sand with big whirly light bulbs on top of it. The light bulbs start whirling around our man Flint and, thanks to the miracle of modern moviemaking, we see him turn into sand right in front of our eyes. The cops show up, Flint isn't there, they scratch their heads, the end.

Not quite.

Here is a guy who is, as he already explained, not a bad person—he's just had bad luck. Which is true, to a point. Yet he still chose to break the law. Yes, his reasons were honorable—he wanted to bring healing to his daughter—but he still broke the law, and that landed him in jail. Although his desires were ultimately good, he went about trying to achieve them in a wrong way, and it nearly cost his life when he fell into that particle accelerator.

And even though his flesh is decimated by that strange nighttime experiment, his desires remain.

In what is, in our opinion, the most poetic and artistic sequence in the entire *Spider-Man* filmography, we are treated to a visually stunning representation of Flint's ascendance as the Sandman. Starting with just a few grains, we see the sand begin to take on a life of its own, flowing in various streams toward each other, almost like water (indeed, there is a nice little crashing wave effect at one point). We see Flint struggling, struggling, struggling to pull these grains together into a meaningful shape.

His body keeps breaking apart. With great effort, he assumes a human-like shape, pulsing, rising out of the mound of sand. His hands are more like big paws, and the rest of him is mere outline.

And then, miraculously, he sees something glinting in the sand. Something that has remained unchanged by the particle accelerator.

The locket.

His desire.

It's the locket that Penny, his daughter, gave to him. He reaches for it with his sandy mitt. He can't close the block-like appendage over the locket, and his body breaks into a big pile of sand, while the locket remains half-buried in the mound.

Congratulations to the visual effects artists who worked on this sequence, for wringing genuine emotion and downright *art* out of a bunch of pixels. Because we now see determination spread across Flint's sandy face. He reaches out his arm again, and this time, he wills it to take a more human shape. Instead of big boxing-glove-like hands, he forces the form of actual fingers and reaches, gingerly, to retrieve the locket.

This is all he needs. Summoning deep desire from within his very soul, Flint finishes the job, staggering out of the pit looking completely like his old self.

We hope we aren't taken to task for this—because there are obvious pitfalls with the comparison we're about to make—but there are many parallels between the rise of the Sandman and the death and resurrection of Jesus Christ.

Okay, okay. First things first: *Jesus was not a villain*. Of course. We know that. We're not saying He was. We hope you're able to look past the obvious contradiction and see this scene from the movie for what it is: an astonishing portrayal of one person miraculously struggling to resurrect himself, whose guiding motivation is love for his child.

Jesus came to this earth out of love. He was sent out of love. God loves us like crazy—more than we love ourselves. Romans 8:38-39 tells us about His love, about how expansive it is:

> For I am convinced that neither death nor life, neither
> angels nor demons, neither the present nor the future,
> nor any powers, neither height nor depth, nor anything
> else in all creation, will be able to separate us from the
> love of God that is in Christ Jesus our Lord.

There is not a thing in this world that can take God's love away from us. Even if our lives feel like they've been smashed to bits by the whirling light bulbs of an experimental particle accelerator. Even if this existence feels like nothing more than a conglomeration of a few million grains of sand. And even if we *deserve* all that—God is still faithful in His love for us.

How can we know? Because Jesus proved it on the cross. He endured the greatest humiliation that has ever been endured; He suffered the greatest shame that has ever been suffered. What Jesus experienced as He died had never been experienced by anyone up to that point in history and has never been duplicated again. He hung on the cross as a condemned criminal; an innocent man wrongly condemned. That was not so unusual. What made His experience unparalleled was that He was executed for every crime that had been committed or ever would be committed. Jesus is the ultimate Judge, yet He hung in the place of all criminals. The enormity of hell opened up and unleashed its full fury on the One who created hell—and heaven. And Jesus took all of this willingly. It was a singular event that has no equal.

And then, after three days, He came back to life. Victorious. Whole. Clean. He brought Himself low, submitted Himself to death . . . and then beat the pants off it to be resurrected. And His motivation?

Love.

Love for you.

Love for His child.

The next time you watch Flint Marko's resurrection scene in *Spider-Man 3*, think about that love—the love of Jesus. Think about how He fought for you. Watch it as a portrayal of His love for you. Watch, and be amazed.

There are no limits to the love Jesus has for you.

CHAPTER TWENTY-ONE

LETTERS FROM A FATHER

She was raised in a less-than-perfect home. Her father, a frustrated writer, was an alcoholic and abused her mom, her older sister and her. What left the deepest scars were his words: "You're just trash, and you'll always be trash."

So when Mary Jane Watson—aspiring actress and the girlfriend of the city's greatest hero, Spider-Man—appears as the lead in a Broadway production, she feels that she has finally overcome her past and has reached her dreams.

Then she reads the comments of a critic who gave her performance a negative review.

"It's just . . . I look at these words, and it's like my father wrote them."

Mary Jane is torn apart by what others think, speak and write about her. But isn't that to be expected? Who wouldn't be hurt by negative words? Or is there more to her reaction than simply the cutting words of a critic?

Mary Jane appears to have what counselors call "approval addiction," a condition similar to codependency. The symptoms of approval addiction include:

- Perfectionism, or working extra hard to make everything just right.
- Conflict avoidance—giving in to others rather than standing for what you believe to be right.
- Poor decision-making skills. Thus, those with approval addiction spend much of their time thinking rather

than doing—you don't want to do it wrong, so you don't do anything at all.

- Trouble expressing emotions, especially anger.

- Lack of self-confidence; constantly needing others to say, "You are doing a good job."

- Trouble telling the truth—will often tell lies for convenience rather than speak the truth that might cause a conflict.

- Fearful of rejection more than anything else.

Do you see Mary Jane in any of the above? How about yourself? Could it be that you, like Mary Jane Watson, have an unhealthy need for approval from others? Some doctors feel that codependency, or approval addiction, is an epidemic in our culture today. How does one become codependent?

Studies show that approval addiction is often handed down from generation to generation within families. For instance, if your grandmother was codependent, chances are good that your mom or dad picked up some of those characteristics and are now passing them on to you. If you have felt a rejection within your family for how you act or what you believe, you could be a candidate for codependency. And if you feel that you must follow a list of "dos" and "don'ts" in order to please your parents—or God—then you are already showing signs of codependency. Those who come from families where one or both parents struggle with alcohol or drug abuse are prime candidates for approval addiction.

Just like Mary Jane Watson. Her father never became a big-time author. He finds himself stuck in a low-paying, dead-end teaching job, and to blur his misery he reaches for a bottle most every night. Instead of taking responsibility for his life and those in his care, he lashes out at his daughter, calling her horrible names. Sticks and stones may break our bones, but names reach to our very souls, scarring us for life.

Mary Jane carries on the cycle, living her life trying to win approval from others. And when she doesn't, she falls further into despair. To escape the state of despair, she works harder to gain approval. And so on. Many of us may be able to ignore the cutting comments of a critic, but not someone with approval addiction. Not Mary Jane Watson.

But there is hope. Let's go back to the beginning, where we see Mary Jane devastated by what she reads in the paper. She says to Peter, "It's just . . . I look at these words, and it's like my father wrote them."

The words her father spoke to her, words that made Mary Jane feel worthless, are still shaping her life. They have carved a deep ditch that she cannot get out of on her own. This is how damaging harsh words spoken by those we love and trust can be.

But there is Someone whose words can overcome the damage done in our lives. His words both *to* us and *about* us can lift us out of our ditch and put us on firm, unshakable ground.

His words are found in the Bible.

Our heavenly Father has spoken about us and to us through the Bible. These are words of life, not of despair and destruction. Read the following words and, where possible, put your own name into the verse to personalize the message.

For I know the thoughts that I think toward you, says the LORD, thoughts of peace and not of evil, to give you a future and a hope (Jeremiah 29:11, *NKJV*).

For I am persuaded that neither death nor life, nor angels nor principalities nor powers, nor things present nor things to come, nor height nor depth, nor any other created thing, shall be able to separate us from the love of God which is in Christ Jesus our Lord (Romans 8:38-39, *NKJV*).

Now thanks be to God, who always leads us in triumph in Christ (2 Corinthians 2:14, *NKJV*).

But God, who is rich in mercy, because of His great love with which He loved us, even when we were dead in trespasses, made us alive together with Christ (by grace you have been saved), and raised us up together, and made us sit together in the heavenly places in Christ Jesus (Ephesians 2:4-6, *NKJV*).

I can do all things through Christ who strengthens me (Philippians 4:13, *NKJV*).

And my God shall supply all your need according to His riches in glory by Christ Jesus (Philippians 4:19, *NKJV*).

Behold what manner of love the Father has bestowed on us, that we should be called children of God! (1 John 3:1, *NKJV*).

These are the words our Father has written to you, about you. Toss away the negative reviews written by the world, by your enemy the devil, and focus on these words. The words of life. The words of your Father.

HUMILITY AND HUMILIATION

One of the most interesting themes that run throughout the *Spider-Man* trilogy is that of our hero fighting "the battle within" (as the marketing campaign for *Spider-Man 3* shouted from the rooftops). Embodied by the symbiotic black suit, Peter's selfishness begins to run amok, feeding, evermore unchecked, on Peter's own fascination with everyone's love for Spider-Man.

But things take a turn for the darker when Peter uses the black suit to seek out revenge on Flint Marko, culminating in that bone-jarring battle within the subterranean world of underground trains (which is probably way more spacious in the film than in real life, but hey—these *are* movies). Peter feeds on his desire for vengeance, and the fun-loving Spidey we've come to know disappears under that thin veneer of black latex.

This Spider-Man is out for blood. Or mud, as the case might be.

Spider-Man discovers that the Sandman has difficulty with water, and winds up gushing him out a sewer grate, eradicating the man who Peter has been told killed his Uncle Ben.

Having successfully fed his bloodlust, Peter changes up his hairstyle to complement his new black duds. He chucks the suit for a while, but after Mary Jane breaks up with him (under the threat of Harry, you'll recall), Peter unleashes the suit once more—and his newfound need for vengeance. This time, he beats up Harry—his one-time best friend—in his own house, detonating that pumpkin bomb in his face and walking away victorious.

And cocky. He starts to wear the suit more and more, taking out rival photographer Eddie Brock (who will become Venom) while he's at it. Yeah, this is feeling good. Why, he might even need to incorporate some dance moves into this.

Which leads to Peter's ill-fated expedition to the Jazz Room with Gwen Stacy, where he shows up everyone on the dance floor. (Say what you will about this intentionally campy sequence, which was either loved or hated by moviegoers, but it serves a purpose in the larger narrative of the film. Whether it serves that purpose well is up for debate, but it does have a reason to exist.) With his little piano-and-dance, Peter loses much of his humanity, using Gwen's heart to club Mary Jane's. He goes to talk to Mary Jane, and Tobey Maguire's eyes become windows into the soul of Peter Parker, allowing us to see "the battle within." It's something to do with the suit, surely. He's feeling confident . . . though maybe a little bit of decency is creeping back into his vengefulness.

A brawl ensues, and as Peter lays waste to the many bouncers at the Jazz Club, he backhands Mary Jane in the process, sending her sprawling to the floor.

"Who *are* you?" she asks.

His transformation is complete, and his life is now destroyed.

It's amazing the depths to which Peter has fallen. Amazing, but not surprising. Because we know from the words of the Bible that the moment we start focusing on ourselves, the minute we believe ourselves awesome, we are courting big-time trouble.

Take, for example, the words of wisdom we find in Proverbs 16:17-18: "The highway of the upright avoids evil; he who guards his way guards his life. Pride goes before destruction, a haughty spirit before a fall."

You want destruction? You want a fall? You want an unguarded life? Just start digging on some pride. It's a surefire way to bring on disaster, a fall from which no amount of genetically modified spider-webbing shooting from your wrists will save you.

Don't believe it? Let's scour the New Testament, starting with Galatians 6:8: "The one who sows to please his sinful nature, from that nature will reap destruction; the one who sows to please the Spirit, from the Spirit will reap eternal life."

How about Philippians 3:17-20?

> Join with others in following my example, brothers, and take note of those who live according to the pattern we gave you. For, as I have often told you before and now say again even with tears, many live as enemies of the cross of Christ. Their destiny is destruction, their god is their stomach, and their glory is their shame. Their mind is on earthly things. But our citizenship is in heaven.

That's just a sample of the Bible's many encouragements to chuck pride in the trash can where it belongs and approach our lives with humility. Peter Parker, in the throes of the symbiotic suit, does all he can to humiliate his foes instead of approaching them in humility. Eddie Brock says as much when he has Spider-Man pinned against the oily web of Venom, Mary Jane dangling in that taxi cab. "You humiliated me," Eddie says, "now I'm going to humiliate you."

Humiliation breeds only humiliation and pride breeds only destruction—a lesson Peter learned all too well. It remains to be seen whether the humiliation Peter doles out will destroy his relationship with Mary Jane beyond repair (though *Spider-Man 3* closes on a hopeful note, indicating that everything's going to be okay between them).

Although Peter's pride opened his life to destruction, the good thing is this: You can almost always rebuild. Doing so takes time, determination and a lot of work. It's much better if you don't go through the destruction in the first place. Determine instead not to let pride rule—and ruin—your life. Seek humility instead.

VENGEANCE BREEDS
VENGEANCE

Vengeance. It's the main thread running through *Spider-Man 3*. Of course, Harry Osborn taps on the window of revenge quite a bit throughout *Spider-Man 2*, but he never really breaks through to the other side until, quite literally, he breaks through the mirror and discovers his father's lab, with this exhortation from his father: *Avenge me.*

Harry first acts on his vengeance by attacking Peter on the street, in that marvelous action-set piece involving Harry in full-on New Goblin gear and Peter in a suit holding a wedding ring. After his unfortunate bout with amnesia, and at the behest of his pops, Harry decides to attack Peter's heart by orchestrating the break-up of Peter and Mary Jane. And then he and Peter get into that big fight in Harry's house, set to the jazz bass line . . . and Harry winds up with smokin' good looks, thanks to a Goblin grenade.

Peter wreaks his share of vengeance in *Spider-Man 3* as well. In addition to caving in to the desires of the symbiote by beating the tar out of Harry and crushing Mary Jane's heart in that campy dance sequence, he destroys the Sandman, thinking that he's killed the man who murdered his Uncle Ben in cold blood.

After taking out Flint Marko, Peter stashes the black suit and pays a visit to Aunt May to tell her the news. He has a trace of a smile on his face as he tells her, very quietly, "Flint Marko, the man who killed Uncle Ben . . . he was killed last night." It's almost as if Peter is expecting Aunt May to break out into delighted joy at the thought of vengeance having been served. But he's a little premature in his celebration.

Peter is unprepared for Aunt May's actual reaction, which is sad shock.

Vengeance has a way of coloring our perception of others. Because we're looking through the eyes of vengeance, we think we're seeing one thing when we're actually seeing something completely different. We're blind to the truth. We've been blinded by our own vengeful hearts.

"What happened?" Aunt May asks reverently.

"Spider-Man killed him," Peter says, the pride apparent in his voice.

"Spider-Man?" Aunt May says. "I don't understand."

Peter's face goes blank. This was not the response he was expecting. Vengeance has gotten in his way.

"Spider-Man doesn't *kill* people," Aunt May continues. "What happened?" she asks again, this time more insistently.

Peter stumbles around for words, starting and restarting his response, never getting past the first syllable. Finally, he drops the poker face and allows his amused bewilderment to show through. "I thought that you'd feel . . ." He trails off, not really wanting to finish the sentence, maybe realizing that the word "happy" would be a highly inappropriate ending.

"He deserved it, didn't he?" Peter asks, truthfully, honestly asking the question. He's not trying to convince Aunt May of anything—he really believes Flint Marko deserved to die.

"I don't think it's for us to say whether a person *deserves* to live or die," Aunt May replies, and we can tell she means it. This isn't something she's just saying—it's a firm conviction.

"But, Aunt May, he killed Uncle Ben," Peter says, as if she doesn't quite comprehend that fact.

But she remains undeterred. "Uncle Ben meant the world to us, but he wouldn't want us living one *second* with revenge in our hearts. It's like a poison. It can take you over. Before you know it . . . turns us into something ugly."

The look on Peter's face as Aunt May unspools the basic theme of the film is priceless. She's just described *him*, under the influence of the black suit, and we can see that he's greatly affected. Unfortunately, Peter's worst behavior is yet to come (we're going to say that detonating the pumpkin bomb in Harry's face and leaving him for dead is worse than spraying the Sandman with several tons of water). We still have a good half-hour, maybe 45 minutes, of Peter living out his various revenge fantasies.

But Aunt May is right—revenge *is* like a poison. And it's taking over our sweet, good-natured Peter Parker and replacing him with a much darker, selfish version. Slowly, Peter's better tendencies are being poisoned by his thirst for vengeance, and the more he allows it—the more he nurses his hurts and tries to heal them with revenge—the darker and colder he gets.

The point, as we see it, is that revenge is only a way to tragedy. Let's look at the lives that Peter's vengeful actions impact:

- He intentionally chooses to take Flint Marko's life. No, his attempt doesn't pan out, but he intends to kill Sandman. For a time, Peter Parker is a murderer.

- He lets a misunderstanding with Mary Jane get out of control, opening the door for Harry to wield his own brand of vengeance and nearly ruin their relationship. Then, Peter yields to his worst instincts, using Gwen Stacy's affection to wound Mary Jane deeply and striking her in anger.

- He intentionally ruins Eddie Brock's career, thereby lending a hand in the creation of his ultimate nemesis, Venom.

- He conducts a Battle Royale with Harry that ends with a bomb and a possibly dead best friend. Perhaps Peter doesn't intend to kill Harry, but he certainly shows very little concern for Harry's life.

All for what? For a little revenge.

Yes, Peter Parker has a lot of reasons to seek vengeance. Flint Marko did, in fact, kill his uncle. Mary Jane does, in fact, hurt him when she breaks up with him (why she doesn't just tell Peter what is going on is a mystery—he is, after all, Spider-Man; if anyone can handle Harry, he can). Eddie Brock does, in fact, resort to treachery and manipulation to wrangle the photography job away from Peter. Harry does, in fact, seek to exact revenge against Peter.

But let's look at what the Bible has to say about the subject, in Romans 12:17-21:

> Do not repay anyone evil for evil. Be careful to do what is right in the eyes of everybody. If it is possible, as far as it depends on you, live at peace with everyone. Do not take revenge, my friends, but leave room for God's wrath, for it is written: "It is mine to avenge; I will repay," says the Lord. On the contrary: "If your enemy is hungry, feed him; if he is thirsty, give him something to drink. In doing this, you will heap burning coals on his head." Do not be overcome by evil, but overcome evil with good.

This exhortation seems to counter logic. How can we possibly be expected to feed our hungry enemies? How can we give them something to drink (and *not* by opening up a big pressurized water pipe and deluging their sandiness with forceful gallons)?

God cares more about the state of our hearts than anything else. And, like Uncle Ben, He doesn't want us to live for a *second* with revenge in our hearts. God wants to spare us the tragedy of revenge. Because when we react to hurt with vengefulness, we're essentially saying we don't believe that God is going to take care of us. We don't believe that He is just. He must have been lying when He said, "It is mine to avenge; I will repay."

We have to believe that God knows what He's doing, and that it isn't up to us to take our revenge on those who hurt us. It doesn't make sense to our natural minds, but when we look at it from a supernatural point of view, it makes perfect sense. Leaving those hurts up to God relieves us of the all-too-weighty responsibility of taking care of them. We can't do anything about the hearts of those who hurt us—we can only take care of our own hearts.

Otherwise, we're taking the fate of the world into our own hands. We're telling God, "It's okay—I got this." We're thumbing our nose at the Creator of the universe and saying, "What You're doing isn't good enough—I need something else, something that I perceive to be better than anything You can offer."

How vain.

Guard your heart well. Look at Peter Parker's story in *Spider-Man 3* as a cautionary tale. And if you find yourself giving in to revenge, take it to God and let Him heal you.

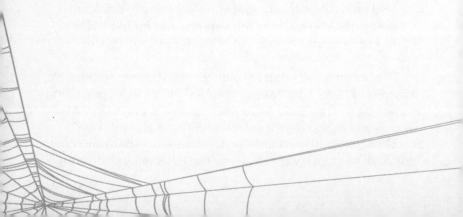

FORGIVE YOURSELF

Forgiveness. Such an easy thing to say; such a difficult thing to offer. It's difficult to offer forgiveness to others when they've wronged us; it's often even *more* difficult to offer it to *ourselves*.

In *Spider-Man 3*, we see the effects on Peter Parker/Spider-Man of withholding forgiveness, when he seeks revenge on Flint Marko/Sandman and when he humiliates Eddie Brock in the newspaper offices. But Peter cannot forgive others until he forgives himself.

Mary Jane has just dumped him. Then he finds out that Harry is the "other man." We see Peter in the shower, and we can imagine that he is trying to wash away all of his hurts. Then he is slumped against the wall of his apartment. When there is a knock on the door, he can hardly pull himself up to answer.

Have you ever felt like you just can't go any farther? Do you sometimes feel as if you were trying to push a boulder uphill? (Read up on the myth of Sisyphus and see if you don't relate.) Then you know how Peter feels at this time in his life.

Depression is just one sign that someone is holding a grudge against himself. Other indicators include frequent outbursts of anger and rage (or outburst's cousin, a lack of any emotion), making insulting comments about himself, and self-abusive behaviors. When you are angry with someone else, you might treat her with disrespect. The same thing occurs when you are mad at yourself.

The solution is fairly simple, but hard to actually do.

Peter gets up and answers the door. After a battle with the perpetually broken doorknob, Peter sees that his visitor is Aunt

May. Just as her grace and beauty are in contrast with the drabness of Peter's cluttered apartment, her kindness in word and action clashes with Peter's self-demeaning words and attitude.

"I never heard from you," says Aunt May. "Did you ever propose?"

Peter shakes his head. "You said, a husband has to put his wife ahead of himself," he says. "I'm not ready for that." He hands Aunt May the ring—her very own wedding ring that she'd given to him in the beginning of the film.

"But what happened?" asks Aunt May. "You seemed so sure."

"I, uh . . ." Peter hesitates and moves away. "I hurt her, Aunt May. I don't know what to do."

The wise, kind and gracious May shares with Peter a word we all need to hear when we are experiencing self-anger: "You start by doing the hardest thing: You forgive yourself."

Peter doesn't feel as though he deserves forgiveness from anyone, not even himself. But if he does not come to grips with his need for forgiveness, he will not be able to do what is needed next: rescuing Mary Jane from Venom.

Forgiving yourself is necessary, even essential, to living an emotionally healthy life. Maybe you are readily able to forgive others when they wrong you, but you can't—or won't—forgive yourself when you do wrong. Perhaps you think that what you have done is so bad and the price that needs to be paid so high that there is no way to earn forgiveness for yourself.

What does God have to say about our sins and what we should do about them? We read in Psalm 103:

God is sheer in mercy and grace; not easily angered, he's rich in love. He doesn't endlessly nag and scold, nor hold grudges forever. He doesn't treat us as our sins deserve, nor pay us back in full for our wrongs. As high as the heaven is over the earth, so strong is his love to those who fear him. And as far as the sunrise is from the sunset, he has separated us from our sins (Psalm 103:8-12, *THE MESSAGE*).

Just how far is the sunrise from the sunset? Well, the sun rises in the east and sets in the west. So we might as well ask, how far is the east from the west? How far do you have to go east before you are now going west? The answer, of course, is infinity. You could travel east indefinitely and never be going in the opposite direction. What the writer of this psalm is saying is this: *When we are forgiven by God, our sins are really gone.* Not just moved to the side to be brought up again at a later date. Gone forever.

Let's look at what God says about our sins through the prophet Jeremiah: "I'll wipe the slate clean for each of them. I'll forget they ever sinned!" (31:34, *THE MESSAGE*). If God is never going to remember our sins again, why do we insist on carrying them around in our heads, in our souls?

Forgiving yourself is not a Vulcan mind-meld trick, a way to block out negative thoughts. It is a recognition that God forgives sins, including yours. Self-forgiveness begins with coming before God, just as we are, to seek His forgiveness. The apostle John wrote:

> If we claim that we are free from sin, we're only fooling ourselves. A claim like that is errant nonsense. On the other hand, if we admit our sins—make a clean break of them—he won't let us down: he'll be true to himself. He'll forgive our sins and purge us of all wrongdoing (1 John 1:8, *THE MESSAGE*).

Self-forgiveness is a two-step process: (1) confess our sins to God and receive His forgiveness; and (2) let go of our guilt inside ourselves. Most of us find the first part easier—much easier—than the second.

In order to let go of your grip on your failures, it may help to talk with someone else. If you don't have an Aunt May in your life, your pastor or youth leader is a good place to start. Then you must trust that God is true to His word: He really will forgive your sins, wipe the slate clean, move them as far as sunrise is to sunset.

Aunt May is right when she tells Peter that forgiving one's self is a hard thing to do. Most of us are harder on ourselves than we are on others. But if we do not take this step, we will not be in a position to rescue others when they call for help. And who knows when Venom may strike next in your life?

Be ready. Forgive yourself.

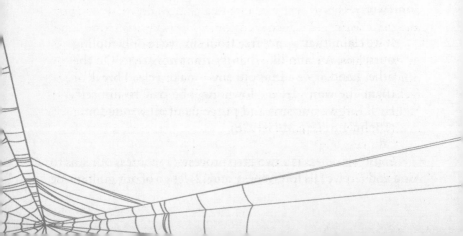

TAKE YOUR SINS TO
THE CROSS

Mary Jane, lying on the floor of the club where she works after being knocked down by a raging Peter Parker, asks perhaps the most important question of the entire Spider-Man series of movies.

"Who *are* you?"

Peter answers honestly: "I don't know . . . I don't know."

Do you know who you are? Do you ever feel out of control, like something has control of you? Do you feel that the symbiotic black suit has become a permanent part of you, that you cannot take it off?

The longer we wear the black costume, the harder it is to take it off. And the harder it is to get off, the more it takes us over and keeps us from being truly ourselves.

Peter gets a clue about what has taken him over, keeping him from being who he really is, when he glances down at his chest and sees the top of his Spidey costume. The *black* Spidey costume.

We have already seen how the symbiote finds a willing host in Peter Parker and how, once it forms the black suit, it gives Spider-Man the sense of greater power—which leads to stronger feelings of hate, arrogance and vengeance. Once we let sin have an inch, it will take a yard of our hearts. It will become a body of death that we must carry wherever we go. Is there a way out?

"Who *are* you?"

Mary Jane's question echoes in Peter's mind as he stands outside of the club in the rain. At first he looks down at the ground, ashamed of what he has done and who he has become. Then he looks up and sees . . . a gothic church steeple topped by a cross. And the next time we see Spidey, he is perched on the side of the steeple, under the cross.

This is more than just symbolic imagery or heavy-handed direction from Sam Raimi. It is truth. The only place where we can become free from the grip of the symbiote, from the hold sin has on us, is under the cross. It is on the cross that our freedom from sin was purchased.

This is not just some religious-sounding expression. According to Old Testament law, when the people of Israel sinned, they had to offer an animal sacrifice, spilling its blood on an altar, in order to be forgiven. The appointed High Priest was constantly making sacrifices for the sins of the people, because they, like us, had a habit of abandoning God in favor of themselves.

As Jesus hung by nails on the cross, His blood poured down the wood all the way to the ground. It was by this blood sacrifice that God declared our sins dealt with once and for all. If that is not great news, then what is?

Is Spider-Man thinking about Jesus' sacrifice as he clings to the church steeple? We don't know. But we next see Spidey going into the bell tower to try to pry the suit free. He has changed his mind about the black suit; it may give him more power, but it has changed him in ways he does not like. So now, instead of being enamored with the black Spidey suit, he realizes that it is wrong for him to wear it.

This "change of mind" has a different name: "repentance." When we hear the word "repent," we may think it means to become a better person, to clean ourselves up. But that is as impossible as it is for Spider-Man to pull the symbiote suit off of himself. If we could take care of our own sin problem, why did God need to sacrifice His own Son on the cross?

No, we can no more clean ourselves up sufficiently to please God than Peter can be his normal, humble self while clad in black. But we *can* change the way we think about our sins. When we admit that our thoughts, words or actions are against the plan God has given us, when we stop thinking we're cruising and realize we're stuck in mud, we are repenting. We are changing our minds about sin. And this is the beginning of the end of the symbiote.

In the sanctuary of that same church, Eddie Brock is praying. He comes to God, he says, humbled and humiliated. He has but one request.

"I want You to kill Peter Parker."

And in a way, Eddie's prayer is answered. Spider-Man, trying to pull the suit of black goo off of his body, stumbles against the church bell; the sound begins to vibrate the symbiote free. The more the bell rings, the more Spidey is able to pull away the goo. Finally he lies in the shadow of the cross, naked but free.

His sinful self is now dead. It has been killed by the power of the cross. The apostle Paul related his own similar death in Galatians 2:20: "I have been crucified with Christ and I no longer live, but Christ lives in me. The life I live in the body, I live by faith in the Son of God, who loved me and gave himself for me."

Our choice is similar to that of Peter/Spidey: We can remain clothed in a costume that smothers the real us and that will, in the end, overtake us completely. Or we can come to the cross, change our minds about wearing the suit and have it peeled (or should we say "pealed"?) off. We may at first be ashamed of our nakedness, but soon God will clothe us—not with a costume, but with garments of salvation, purchased at the ultimate cost (see Isaiah 61:10).

THE LORD'S PRAYER . . .
NOT EDDIE'S

There he was: a humbled, humiliated man. He'd made some grand mistakes, yes, but did he really deserve this? Sure, he'd completely thumbed his nose at the concept of journalistic integrity in the pursuit of his own career . . . and maybe he'd stepped on a few little people on the way up . . . but did Eddie Brock *really* deserve to be fired and ostracized?

Well . . . yes.

Nevertheless, like many others before him who found themselves at rock bottom, Eddie turns to God for a solution. He approaches the cathedral with reverence, dipping his fingers into the holy water and genuflecting with all appropriate veneration.

He kneels in the empty cathedral and begins to address God:

"It's Brock, Sir." Good start, that. Calling God "Sir" can never hurt.

"Edward Brock, Jr." Just in case God didn't know who he was.

"I come before You today," Eddie says, pausing to choose the right words, the emotional wounds apparent as he struggles to get them out, "humbled . . . and humiliated . . . to ask You for one thing."

This is good. This is a good way to start a prayer: acknowledging your own weakness and God's strength. Not bad, not bad at all. Ask away, my son.

"I want You to kill Peter Parker."

You can almost hear the needle scratching across the record. Do *what*? You don't have to be a super-Christian to know that

Eddie's heart is totally in the wrong place. Sort of crossing the line there, Eddie.

But what kind of prayer *should* Eddie have prayed? We find the answer in Matthew 6, in what has come to be known as "the Lord's Prayer." In this passage, Jesus was holding forth on a variety of topics, preaching about this and that, and these are His thoughts on the subject of prayer. Let's start with verses 5-8:

> And when you pray, do not be like the hypocrites, for they love to pray standing in the synagogues and on the street corners to be seen by men. I tell you the truth, they have received their reward in full. But when you pray, go into your room, close the door, and pray to your Father, who is unseen. Then your Father, who sees what is done in secret, will reward you. And when you pray, do not keep on babbling like pagans, for they think they will be heard because of their many words. Do not be like them, for your Father knows what you need before you ask him.

So far, so good. No, Eddie isn't in his room, but he isn't on the street corner trying to show off with his prayer; the cathedral he's in is empty, except for the priest walking around in there (well, and Peter about to start stumbling about in the bell tower). Eddie doesn't "keep on babbling like pagans," but keeps his prayer short and sweet. It would appear that he's on the right track.

Let's keep going and see what Jesus has to say in verses 9-13:

> This, then, is how you should pray: "Our Father in heaven, hallowed be your name, your kingdom come, your will be done on earth as it is in heaven. Give us today our daily bread. Forgive us our debts, as we also have forgiven our debtors. And lead us not into temptation, but deliver us from the evil one."

Let's see . . . Eddie gets the first part *sort of* right. That "Sir" he throws in at the beginning is at least respectful, even if it's not an outright "Father in heaven, hallowed be Your name, Your kingdom come, Your will be done on earth as it is in heaven." We'll just assume that's what he means by "Sir."

We can also assume that Eddie's concept of "daily bread" is "kill Peter Parker," which is . . . not quite right. Revenge isn't really something you can chow down on, every day. It *is* something that a lot of people try to feed themselves, but it is never satisfying. Rather, it's a destructive force that only kills you the more you feed on it. Sort of like trying to quench your thirst with paint thinner.

Moving on, we come to another troublesome part: "Forgive us our debts as we also have forgiven our debtors." Perhaps Eddie doesn't really feel like he has any debts that need to be forgiven, and is therefore off the hook when it comes to this particular part of the prayer. Perhaps.

But then, blowing that notion out of the water, Jesus gives us verses 14-15: "For if you forgive men when they sin against you, your heavenly Father will also forgive you. But if you do not forgive men their sins, your Father will not forgive your sins." That's pretty cut and dried. If you've messed up—and Eddie knows that he has messed up—then you're in need of forgiveness. And if you're in need of forgiveness, you have to forgive others.

So instead of praying that God will strike down Peter Parker in some sort of grand, Old Testament-style way (perhaps the ground opening up and swallowing him?), Eddie should pray something along the lines of, "It's Brock, Sir. Edward Brock, Jr. I come before You today . . . humbled . . . and humiliated. And I pray that You will help me to forgive Peter Parker for messing up my life so badly."

Something like that would have been good. Not to let Eddie off the hook, because he flouted the rules of journalistic integrity and needs to be disciplined for it. Peter's motivations were improper—he was trying to get Eddie fired out of spite and malice—but his actions were correct. Eddie's deceit needed to be exposed.

But after that happened, Eddie *still* needs to forgive Peter. Because he needs forgiveness himself. Eddie needs to look to the model prayer Jesus gave us in Matthew 6:5-15 and determine how it applies to his life and situation—before he goes into that cathedral to pray. Because not only does his prayer *not* get answered while he is in there, but the very thing that had influenced Peter to expose Eddie—the symbiote—attaches itself to him. Eddie becomes what he despised in Peter.

All because of a selfish prayer.

It's sometimes tempting to twist our prayers to meet our own concerns. To go to God and say, "But they really hurt me, so can You make them pay a little, please?" But that just isn't the type of prayer that will get heard. When we pray like that, we're merely exposing our own shortcomings.

Instead, when you pray, use the Lord's Prayer as your model. And if you have trouble with that, just remember the prayer Jesus offered in the Garden of Gethsemane, moments before He was captured, just hours before He went to the cross: "My Father, if it is possible, may this cup be taken from me. Yet not as I will, but as you will" (Matthew 26:39). That's simple enough. State your request, then fall back on this: Not my will, God, but Yours. Here's what I want, but if that goes against what *You* want, then I'll do what *You* want instead.

That's the type of prayer God wants to hear. Try it out and see what happens.

NO GREATER LOVE

It's safe to say that Harry Osborn and Peter Parker have some . . . issues . . . between them. What with all the Mary Jane dating . . . and the mix-up with Harry thinking Spider-Man killed his father . . . and then, you know, the thrilling battle between them that opens up *Spider-Man 3* . . . and then their fight later on, when Peter has on the black suit and explodes that bomb in Harry's face and leaves him for dead.

Issues. Yeah.

But Peter does what he can to put those issues aside, to bring some healing to their lives, when he goes to Harry toward the climax of the film. The Sandman and Venom have Mary Jane trapped in that taxi 80 stories in the air.

"I need your help," Peter tells Harry. "I can't take them both, not by myself."

Harry reveals his scarred face, with his wonky eyeball. "You don't deserve my help."

"She needs us," Peter implores.

"Get out."

Still some issues there. But, thanks to the über-butler Bernard, things get put back on track, and Harry finally knows the truth: that his father died of his own accord, not because of Peter. "I loved your father," Bernard says, "as I have loved you. As your friends have loved you."

So now it's time for Harry to internalize Bernard's words and show his love for his friends. Peter's already heading toward the scene of the crime to rescue his girl. It doesn't go very well (though Spider-Man does get a chance to holler "Hold on, Mary

Jane!" for, like, the fiftieth time in the trilogy). The pair of villains are just too much for Spidey to handle, and soon he is held down against an I-beam by Venom as the Sandman pounds the patooey out of him.

Yes, as the news announcer helpfully intones, "This could be the end of Spider-Man."

But wait! What's this tiny orangey-gold dot approaching from off-camera, embedding into the Sandman's neck with a tiny *plop*? Why, it's a pumpkin bomb! It must be from Harry! And as it blows a gaping, flaming crater in the giant Sandman's head, we see that, yes! Harry, as the New Goblin, is coming to the rescue on his hoverboard!

Yea, forgiveness!

Having temporarily disabled the Sandman, Harry gives Venom the old one-two with the sides of his hoverboard, rescuing Spider-Man from certain death-by-pounding. With a smirk and a pithy line, the formerly on-the-outs best friends are now allies against their enemies, and the posterior-kicking begins in earnest.

Things happen, a lot of pixels wage war against each other, and then Spidey gets hammered by the Sandman, falling right into the clutches of Venom. Peter tries to convince Eddie to let go of the suit, but Eddie isn't having it. As Venom, Eddie is prepared to deliver the death blow . . . when Harry shows up to spoil the party, armed with nifty blade things on the front of his hoverboard.

But Harry is tossed aside, his hoverboard falling into the bad guy's hands . . . and the stage is set: Venom raises the hoverboard above his head and springs. The end of Spider-Man is near. It's only a matter of time.

And then there's Harry. Stepping between Peter and his nemesis, he takes the blade intended for his friend.

Just like that, Harry is mortally wounded.

The moment is rich with meaning. In this selfless act, Harry showcases his love for his friend, Peter. That he is killed by the blade of his own glider—which is exactly the way his father died, though in different circumstances—only adds to the poignancy.

Combine with this scene a statement from Jesus, found in John 15:13:

> Greater love has no one than this, that he lay down his life for his friends.

Harry's sacrifice is a moving illustration of Jesus' words. With his acts of heroism—coming to Peter's aid, not once but twice, then stepping in front of the blades meant to end his friend's life—Harry demonstrates the greatest love possible.

When Jesus spoke those words, He spoke them in this context: "My command is this: Love each other as I have loved you. Greater love has no one than this, that he lay down his life for his friends." That's the same passage as before, but with verse 12 added. And what a difference that verse 12 makes.

With that preceding verse, we see that, when Jesus talked about laying down one's life for a friend, He was talking about *Himself*. That's what He meant when He said "as I have loved you." This was a Man who was about to lay down His life, willingly, for His friends . . . for those He loves. He sacrificed His life so that we could *live*.

In a way, Harry does the same thing—though his sacrifice doesn't purchase eternal life and redemption for his friend Peter Parker. But it does allow Peter to live, and to live abundantly. Peter is motivated by Harry's death to defeat Venom, and then follows Harry's model of forgiveness by forgiving Flint Marko a few minutes later.

There really is no greater love than to lay down one's life. It's the love Harry Osborn shows for Peter Parker, and it's the love Jesus showed for us. It's up to us to recognize it, and accept it.

And then show it whenever we can. We don't have to die in a literal sense to show others that same kind of love; we can show it by putting their needs in front of our own. By giving up our personal time to volunteer at church or by buying lunch for someone who can't afford it.

Lay down your life. You'll be surprised at the love you find.

THE UNCONDITIONAL LOVE
OF UNCLE BEN

Peter Parker is not hurting for father figures in his life, though he *is* hurting for father figures that are stable, loving influences. Throughout the *Spider-Man* trilogy, we see Peter surrounded by father-like people: Norman Osborn in film 1, who didn't turn out quite so good; Otto Octavius in film 2, who . . . well, same story, different guy. In all three films, J. Jonah Jameson and Dr. Connors are both father-like figures, influencing Peter in his profession and his schoolwork, respectively.

But the greatest father figure Peter has is the man who most closely resembled a father when Peter was growing up: Uncle Ben. Despite Peter's protestations in the early goings of *Spider-Man*, Uncle Ben *was* his father (and yes, Peter does tell Norman Osborn that realization at the end of the picture). When Uncle Ben dies in the first film, it creates an emotional wound that Peter carries through the rest of the trilogy.

His thirst for revenge makes sense when Captain Stacy tells him that Flint Marko was Uncle Ben's killer (which isn't the case in the comics, but we're talking about the movies here, so just go with it). Peter takes it out on Flint in the subway, but the Sandman rises again to pound the stuffing out of Peter with that big, sandy fist at the construction site. Blah, blah, blah, the battle is finally over, Venom is gone and Peter is standing there, shell-shocked.

"I didn't want this," says a voice behind him. It's Flint. The Sandman.

Then Flint relays the story of what really happened on that street corner that fateful night, and we see a portrait of Uncle Ben that confirms all we know about him. It starts with Flint rapping the barrel of his gun against the window of Uncle Ben's car, and ends with the same barrel of that same gun unloading a bullet into Uncle Ben's abdomen.

In between, Flint ordered Uncle Ben out of the car, telling the older man that he needs the vehicle. Once Uncle Ben is standing on the sidewalk, the kindly old gent lays a hand on Flint's shoulder: "Why don't you just put down the gun and go home?" he asks.

In the midst of this intense moment—a carjacking at the hands of a career thief—Uncle Ben's primary concern isn't his own car or his own life. His primary concern is *Flint*.

"Why don't you just put down the gun and go home?"

The question reveals a lot about Uncle Ben and the way he saw the world. He saw the outside circumstances of the theft, but looked into Flint's soul and saw someone worth rescuing. Uncle Ben loved him.

We know this because the Bible gives us a full, round, beautiful definition of love in 1 Corinthians 13:4-8:

> Love is patient, love is kind. It does not envy, it does not boast, it is not proud. It is not rude, it is not self-seeking, it is not easily angered, it keeps no record of wrongs. Love does not delight in evil but rejoices with the truth. It always protects, always trusts, always hopes, always perseveres. Love never fails.

To cap it off, a few verses later, we have this summary: "And now these three remain: faith, hope, and love. But the greatest of these is love" (v. 13).

Look at the attributes of love in how Uncle Ben dealt with Flint Marko, car-jacker and thief. Uncle Ben was patient with him.

Even when he was hustled out of the car, he retained a demeanor of calm.

He was kind, laying his hand on Flint's shoulder in a gesture of kindness.

He didn't show envy. Envy is selfishness, and in that moment, Uncle Ben's only concern was for Flint.

He didn't boast. Uncle Ben could have laid into Flint, calling him a lowlife and contrasting him from the law-abiding citizen whose car he's stealing. Instead, Ben kept quiet—except for that question, the question that would haunt Flint in prison.

He wasn't rude. He asked his question with sincerity. He presented Flint with an actual option, not a rhetorical question designed to ridicule him.

He wasn't self-seeking. Again, he put aside his own concerns to deal with the bigger question of Flint's behavior.

He wasn't easily angered. Boy, did he have a right to be angry! He was just sitting there, and some dude came up with a gun to take his car. But Ben sidestepped his anger and looked at the bigger picture.

He kept no record of wrongs. He wasn't concerned with Flint's past. His question, "Why don't you just put down the gun and go home?" hinted that the past doesn't matter. Whatever Flint's reasons for being there, he still had a choice; he could put his gun down and go home.

Uncle Ben is a great characterization of love. Not to elevate him to sainthood, because that would be silly (he's not a real person, after all), but in an incredibly tense moment, he acted so much differently than most of us would. Yes, Ben lost his life, but not because he loved. He lost it because of a freak accident.

We are called to love those around us, and it can be a dangerous mission. When we love, we open ourselves up to risk.

Had Uncle Ben hit the sidewalk screaming, he likely would have lived.

But he wouldn't have loved.
Which is worth more to you: your life or your love?

THE CHOICE

It comes to this: Spider-Man, unmasked, facing Sandman atop a half-finished skyscraper. Both are weary. Both are beaten up. Does either of them have the strength or will to fight it out once more?

Sandman apparently has had enough. Instead of attacking, he says, "I didn't want this . . . but I had no choice."

Spidey looks him up and down. Should he spin a web around the Sandman? After all, he *is* a wanted criminal. Or should he renew the battle, strive to finish the dirtbag who killed his uncle Ben? He will be a hero either way.

Spider-Man chooses a third way. He responds, "We always have a choice."

It is a lesson that has taken him the entire movie to learn.

Peter had to choose whether he would pursue his own interests and fulfill his own desires, or learn to put Mary Jane, whom he wanted as his wife, ahead of himself.

He had to choose between confronting Eddie Brock privately about the fake photograph Eddie used to get the job Peter wanted, or to publicly humiliate Eddie in order to get the job himself.

Peter had to choose between the red/blue suit or the black suit.

We always have a choice.

Once Spidey had chosen the black suit—which felt really good and gave him extra strength and more power—the power to choose became much harder. It seemed that the black suit was making all of the choices for him.

He chose to become "cool Peter Parker," dressing hip and becoming arrogant. There really wasn't even a time he made a conscious decision to become that way. Wearing the black suit just made the slide into this "new" Peter all the easier.

We always have a choice.

What is left unsaid, but is plainly seen, is this: Our choices always have consequences. And those consequences affect those close to us as well.

Peter's choice to take Gwen Stacy to the club where Mary Jane was working backfired. Not only did he end up looking like a total jerk—to both Gwen and Mary Jane—he hit the woman he really loved and knocked her to the ground. His choice to get even with his best friend Harry left Harry with scars over half of his face, and even more determination to kill Spider-Man. And his choice to humiliate Eddie Brock ended with Brock taking on the form of Venom, kidnapping and almost killing Mary Jane. That battle cost Harry and Eddie their lives.

Our decisions have consequences that reach far beyond us.

Flint Marko had a choice the night he killed Uncle Ben. He could have not gone out with the intent to steal. He could have done as Uncle Ben suggested—just put down the gun and go home. Even after the fatal shot, he could have stayed to care for Ben and turned himself over to the police. But he made none of these choices. And the consequences set in motion by his decision had far-reaching effects. A family lost a husband and uncle to death. Another family lost a husband and father to prison. And after escaping from prison, Marko—through a freak accident—lost his humanness and became a collection of sand molecules.

So when Flint tells Spider-Man, "I had no choice," he is not looking through the lens of reality. He made choices, and now he—and many others—are living out the consequences.

You have choices in front of you today. What shirt to wear. What to eat for lunch. How to spend that fiver in your pocket.

How to respond to the person who is spreading untrue gossip about you. Whether to cheat on that test, even though you know you probably won't get caught. Whether to react in anger when someone asks you to do something that is inconvenient for you at the moment. Each of these decisions you make will affect many other areas of your life—and the lives of others around you.

You always have a choice.

The key is making a good one. There is no magic formula, no one-two-three to always doing the right thing. It is a daily exercise in giving up control of your life—your choices—to God. We wish this surrender could be a one-time thing and then we would never have to deal with it again. In reality, however, we enter into this battle every day.

Even the man who has been called the wisest person to ever live had to choose who would call the shots in his life: himself or God. King Solomon wrote these words many years ago, and they still hold true for us today:

> Trust God from the bottom of your heart; don't try to figure everything out on your own. Listen for God's voice in everything you do, everywhere you go; He's the one who will keep you on track (Proverbs 3:5-6, *THE MESSAGE*).

That is the key to making good choices: Trust God. He knows how things will turn out even before they begin. He can be counted on to help us make decisions whose consequences are good for everyone.

We always have a choice. True words.

What's the best choice we can make? To trust God.

Always.

THE MOST POWERFUL WEAPON

We've seen quite a few powerful weapons throughout the *Spider-Man* trilogy.

Norman Osborn, as the Green Goblin, has his glider with the rockets and knives, and his bombs, and his little intelligent razor-bird things, and his green sleepy gas that comes out of his wrists.

Otto Octavius, as Doctor Octopus, has smart arms that basically give him powers similar to Spider-Man . . . plus, there are nifty knives tucked away in there.

Harry Osborn, as the New Goblin, has his hoverboard packed with bombs, rockets and knives (and those fire-jet things), and those same intelligent razor-bird things, and those sharp claws or whatever that come out of his forearms, and that green sword that does . . . something.

Flint Marko, as the Sandman, has a bunch of sand . . . which he creatively forms into a variety of weapons of the pummeling kind.

Eddie Brock, as Venom, has some pretty sharp teeth, and nails in need of a manicure, and all the nifty stuff Spider-Man can do.

And Peter Parker, as Spider-Man, has his super-powers—though his only real weapons are his fists, feet and those little batches of webbing he shoots.

So, yeah. Loads of weapons in the films. And that's not counting the many found objects that are used as weapons (pipes, bank vault doors, water, subway trains . . . you get the idea).

But the most powerful weapon we see in the entire film series doesn't show up until six hours into the trilogy, with about 10 minutes left in the whole shebang, including credits.

Before we get to it, let's set the stage: Venom has just been finished off, when Eddie Brock jumps into the fray and is detonated like crazy. As the concussion of the blast wears off, Peter stands unmasked in his Spidey suit, taking it all in.

He drops the pipe to the ground with a clang, and hears a voice from behind him. It's Flint Mark: "I didn't want this . . . but I had no choice."

"We always have a choice," Peter says, his anger beginning to rise again. He's been replaying that black and white movie in his head over and over for days, the one where he imagines how it went down when Flint shot Uncle Ben. In that movie, the one we see, Flint shoots Uncle Ben just for the heck of it. For no reason. Peter has convinced himself that *this* is how it happened. "You had a choice when you killed my uncle."

"My daughter was dying," Flint says, launching into what will become an explanation, not a defense, of what actually happened. "I needed money." He thinks a moment. "I was scared."

Then we see a black and white movie. Not the one Peter has been playing in his head, the one Peter invented, but the one that tells us what *really* happened. Uncle Ben, standing on the sidewalk, trying to convince Flint to give it up and go home . . . David Carradine running toward them with a satchel full of money, reaching out and grabbing Flint's arm . . . the lightning flash of the gun's report . . . Flint's shocked reaction . . . Uncle Ben falling, falling to the ground . . . Carradine taking off to save his own skin . . . Flint immediately remorseful.

"I spent a lot of nights wishing I could take it back," Flint says, back on the rooftop with Peter. He pauses, thinking for a moment, then says (in Thomas Haden Church's gravelly voice—no wonder they cast him as the Sandman), "I'm not asking you to forgive me. I just want you to understand."

Peter struggles to process all this information and his thoughts, finally, turn inward. "I've done terrible things, too," he admits (not mentioning that one of those terrible things was, you know, trying to kill the person he's talking to now). He looks up at Flint, and his expression seems to apologize for trying to take his life.

Flint turns to look down at the fracas below, with all the emergency vehicles and gathered crowds. "I didn't choose to be this," he says. He raises his hand and looks one more time at the locket with the photo of Penny. "The only thing left of me now is my daughter."

Peter stares at him for a long time, then works up the courage to finally say it: "I forgive you."

And there it is. The most powerful weapon in the series.

Spider-Man had tried a multitude of ways to defeat the Sandman. He tried to punch him out in that armored car. He tried to grind him down with a subway train. He tried to drown him. He and Harry tried to pound him into submission with punches, kicks, bombs and rockets. None of these attempts had worked.

The only thing that can end the fighting between Spider-Man and the Sandman is forgiveness.

Jesus had a lot to say about forgiveness. Take, for example, the Parable of the Unmerciful Servant:

Then Peter came to Jesus and asked, "Lord, how many times shall I forgive my brother when he sins against me? Up to seven times?" Jesus answered, "I tell you, not seven times, but seventy-seven times (or seventy times seven). Therefore, the kingdom of heaven is like a king who wanted to settle accounts with his servants. As he began the settlement, a man who owed him ten thousand talents was brought to him. Since he was not able to pay, the master ordered that he and his wife and his children and all that he had be sold to repay the debt.

"The servant fell on his knees before him. 'Be patient with me,' he begged, 'and I will pay back everything.' The servant's master took pity on him, canceled the debt, and let him go.

"But when that servant went out, he found one of his fellow servants who owed him a hundred denarii. He grabbed him and began to choke him. 'Pay back what you owe me!' he demanded.

"His fellow servant fell to his knees and begged him, 'Be patient with me, and I will pay you back.'

"But he refused. Instead, he went off and had the man thrown in prison until he could pay the debt. When the other servants saw what had happened, they were greatly distressed and went and told their master everything that had happened.

"Then the master called the servant in. 'You wicked servant,' he said. 'I canceled all that debt of yours because you begged me to. Shouldn't you have had mercy on your fellow servant just as I had on you?' In anger his master turned him over to the jailers to be tortured, until he should pay back all he owed.

"This is how my heavenly Father will treat each of you unless you forgive your brother from your heart" (Matthew 18:21-35).

Harsh, to say the least. But such is the nature of unforgiveness. If you're going to withhold forgiveness from others when you, yourself, are in need of it, then you're setting yourself up to live by a harsh standard. And if you're going to withhold forgiveness from others, then God is going to withhold it from you. And you really do not want God withholding *anything* from you.

Forgiveness is hard. Especially when someone has really hurt you, as Flint hurt Peter. But if we learn anything from *Spider-Man 3*, it's this: Vengeance offers no consolation, no victory. The only place where we find healing and peace is in a place of forgiveness.

Forgiveness. It's the ultimate weapon.

Wield it well.

REAL-LIFE SUPERHEROES

We, your humble authors, were perusing the Internet while writing this book and stumbled on an incredible story from the Minneapolis/St. Paul City Pages website called "Superheroes in Real Life: Inspired by Comic Books, Ordinary Citizens Are Putting On Masks to Fight Crime."[1]

Written by Ward Rubrecht, the article examines a new trend in superheroism: Reals. There's a movement afoot in society today (albeit small) of average, ordinary citizens who are pulling on some sort of superhero garb and doing good in their communities.

The article begins by following a Real named "Geist"—a middle-aged man who sold off his comic book collection to fund his new life as a superhero—as he suits up in a duster, sunglasses, a wide-brim hat and "green iridescent mask," along with a small assortment of non-lethal weapons like smoke bombs, pepper spray and "an Argentinean cattle-snare."

Why is Geist so geared up? Because he's about to deliver groceries to a local homeless shelter.

Such is the world of Reals, most of whom, as Geist puts it, are "basically normal people who just find an unusual way to do something good." A few Reals are interested in busting the chops of drug dealers they may find, but most of them are just costumed people looking to align with a charity or cause, to lend some panache and publicity to an organization doing a good thing.

It's an interesting idea, especially in light of our discussion here. Because what is Peter Parker if not a representation of us, the average person in the world? And what is Spider-Man if not a representation of what we would all like to be: super?

The great thing is that super deeds need not be limited to the comic book page or to the movie or television screen, as our Real friends point out. And as the apostle Paul pointed out, more than once, in his writings. Take, for example, 1 Corinthians 12:4-20. It's long, but every word packs a punch:

There are different kinds of gifts, but the same Spirit. There are different kinds of service, but the same Lord. There are different kinds of working, but the same God works all of them in all men.

Now to each one the manifestation of the Spirit is given for the common good. To one there is given through the Spirit the message of wisdom, to another the message of knowledge by means of the same Spirit, to another faith by the same Spirit, to another gifts of healing by that one Spirit, to another miraculous powers, to another speaking in different kinds of tongues, and to still another the interpretation of tongues. All these are the work of one and the same Spirit, and he gives them to each one, just as he determines.

The body is a unit, though it is made up of many parts; and though all its parts are many, they form one body. So it is with Christ. For we were all baptized by one Spirit into one body—whether Jews or Greeks, slave or free—and we were all given the one Spirit to drink.

Now the body is not made up of one part but of many. If the foot should say, "Because I am not a hand, I do not belong to the body," it would not for that reason cease to be part of the body. And if the ear should say, "Because I am not an eye, I do not belong to the body," it would not for that reason cease to be part of the body. If the whole body were an eye, where would the sense of hearing be? If the whole body were an ear, where would the sense of smell be? But in fact God has arranged the parts of the body, every one of them, just as he wanted them to be. If they were all one part, where would the body be? As it is, there are many parts, but one body.

Such truth, captured in so few words.

But how does it apply here? Think of it this way: We all have a job to do. We all have a responsibility to this world to try to make it a better place. No, we can't each individually change the world—but if we think of ourselves as all part of the same team, the same body, and we each individually do our own jobs, live out our own callings, then we *can* change the world. We can be super.

It's available. It's up to us.

Peter Parker is just a fictional character. Spider-Man was created by Stan Lee to sell comic books. But, as we have seen, spiritual truth permeates even modern myths—and though we may not have the power that comes from being bitten by a genetically modified spider, we do have super power.

So don't wait for a fluke spider bite. Don't wait for a freak lab accident to infuse you with green gas or to fuse your smart arms to your body. Don't wait to fall into a particle accelerator.

Just take what you have, what God has given you, and be Real.

That's all He asks.

You have great power. The great responsibility to use it is now up to you.

Change the world.

Your friendly neighborhood *you*.

Note

1. Ward Rubrecht, "Superheroes in Real Life: Inspired by Comic Books, Ordinary Citizens Are Putting On Masks to Fight Crime," City Pages, January 15, 2008. Here's the link, if you want to read it for yourself: http://www.citypages.com/2008-01-16/feature/superheroes-in-real-life/full/ (accessed January 2010).

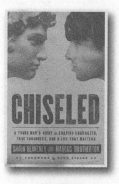
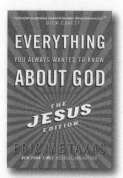